STITCH SAVVY

25 SKILL-BUILDING PROJECTS TO TAKE YOUR SEWING TECHNIQUE TO THE NEXT LEVEL

HOME DÉCOR • PATCHWORK & QUILTING • BAGS • SEWING FOR CHILDREN • CLOTHING

DEBORAH MOEBES

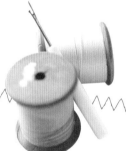

kp

Cincinnati, Ohio

CONTENTS

WELCOME, STITCHERS!

It has been a sincere privilege these past few years to see the sheer numbers of folks drawn to sewing who had never sewn before. Watching so many learn to sew, or re-learn to sew, and become completely smitten with the craft is exciting and motivating and inspiring in a way that I couldn't have predicted. As more and more new stitchers got some real projects under their belts, it became pretty clear that the resources that were out there for someone wanting to sew were mainly divided into two camps: introductory books, like *Stitch by Stitch*, that were designed to help newbies pick up needle and thread and fall in love; and niche books that focused on much more involved techniques, which were designed for experienced stitchers who knew exactly what they were looking for. There wasn't a whole lot in between.

Yet here you are! You've got some sewing experience, you know you love working with fabric and thread and your machine, and you have ideas. You rock. You're still searching for some guidance, though, for someone to lend you a hand and help you find your footing in the midst of the reams of information out there. How do you know when you're ready to move on to more challenging sewing? How do you know what kind of project to do next? When do you use one fabric over another, and how do you take a skill you used with one project and make it useful someplace else? I wanted this book to fill in that gap in the sewing knowledge, and give you a reference that would help you make the leap from Beginner to Rock Star.

As you work through the projects you'll find here, keep in mind that each of them was designed to relate particular skills or techniques. Naturally, not every technique in the whole wide world is covered here, and there are some that show up more than once because I tend to favor them—that doesn't mean there is only one way of doing something. Far from it! What it means is that I hope you will continue your love affair with sewing, that these projects will ignite a passion in you to press ahead and challenge yourself, and that you'll be moved to make something that maybe you didn't ever think you'd make. Sewing has so many amazing discoveries within it—it's my sincere wish that this book will give you the tools to step beyond the basics, rise to a new skill level and march forward until YOU are the one designing the projects the rest of us want to sew!

Let's rock the house, y'all.

It's time to get sewing.

HOW TO USE THIS BOOK

When most folks learn to sew, they have pretty specific projects in mind that they'd like to complete. As I meet each student in my Intro to Sewing classes, I ask them to tell me what brought them to sewing and where they'd like to go next. If learning to sew is their A, what's their B, that sort of thing. What I've learned over and over again is that the majority of us don't want to sew everything, we just want to sew a few things and sew them really well. (It's my dirty secret that I want to coax each and every one of you until you DO want to sew everything, but that's just between you, me and the gatepost, okay?)

Some folks come in and really want to learn to sew in order to decorate their homes. Others are new moms and want to make super cute clothes for their children. Or maybe you're a handbag junkie and just learned that you can make your own custom-designed purses and you're sold on sewing. Whatever it is that attracted you to sewing to begin with, most of us have the tendency to learn the basics and then "track" ourselves, devoting most of our time to one specific family of sewing projects. Most of these fall into one of five categories: home décor, bags, children's items, quilting and apparel.

As you move from being a beginning stitcher to stretching your intermediate wings, I want you to be able to grow your skills step by step, pursue the projects you really crave and test the waters outside your comfort zone—all while having a friendly hand to hold along the way. This book is designed specifically to allow you to do those things, and make some seriously cute projects as you do. Ready?

For each of the five categories of sewing (home décor, handbags, kids' items, quilting and clothing), there are five projects. Each project is more challenging than the one before it, so they're ranked from one to five—one is an entry-level project, two builds on one, three extends beyond that and on until five. Make sense? So, if you're really itching to quilt, start with the first project in the quilting section and work through the fifth.

But wait! There's more! Maybe you really like home décor sewing, but you're curious about making handbags and clothing. Right? Since every project family has five projects that get progressively more advanced, you can do all the Level One projects, then all the Level Two, then all the Level Three—working your way through all five project families and gaining insane skills as you go.

Not convinced? There's even more! (And this is probably my favorite part.) When you're working on a particular project, maybe you find that a specific skill or technique is really appealing to you—like piping or reversibles. As you complete each project, you'll find a sidebar that directs you to related projects throughout the book featuring techniques that you just learned! How cool is that? As you sew your way through the twenty-five projects in these pages, you can Select Your Own Escapade (to avoid stepping on a familiar trademarked phrase from my youth) and jump around the book, choosing a starting point and then choosing the next project as you complete each one. You'll find guidance after every project to lead you to your options as you move ahead, and each one takes into account other skills and techniques you'll want to master! Woot!

Level 1 quilting project

Level 4 quilting project

NEXT STEPS

Take the idea of reversibles to another level—now that you've made this reversible cover, make the **Reversible Girl's Dress** (see page 132). You can even add trim!

The cutting skills you used to make the patchwork inset for this cover will come in super handy as you prep the pieces for the **Travel Matching Game** (see page 144).

All those clean, straight lines of quilting show up again on the **Reversible Quilted Satchel** (see page 112)—what a great place to keep working on perfecting that skill!

At the end of each project, the Next Steps sidebar directs you to other projects in the book that use similar skills.

NEXT STEPS

SEWING BASICS REVIEW: QUICK AND DIRTY

Before jumping into your first project—whether you start at the very beginning and work your way through or decide to jump around through the book and see where the spirit leads you—we'll want to review the skills you've already mastered so our chops are honed and our machines are warmed up and oiled, ready to rock and roll. You ready?

Supplies Review

Theoretically, you already have the basic tools that any well-stocked sewing kit requires. Let's review those, and then add a few more that you'll probably want to include now that you're totally intermediate.

Shears: This is the single most important sewing tool you'll ever own. Invest in a good, all-steel pair and prepare to be amazed (and amazing). These puppies are your bread and butter, so keep them sharp so they cut like butter. I also swear by my 6" (15.2 cm) snips and my tiny embroidery scissors and use all three pair every time I sew.

Iron: Whether you iron in real life or not, you'll need a good-quality iron for pressing your sewing. You might think that any iron is just like any other iron, but you'd be wrong: A good iron is worth its weight in chocolate, and that's not just whistling Dixie. Look for a heavier iron with a stainless steel sole plate, one that has a good steam function.

Seam ripper: Not something to be ashamed of, this bad boy is an eraser for your sewing adventures. Very (very, very, VERY) few sewing projects get all the way through from beginning to end without needing to have a stitch or two removed here and there. Your seam ripper is perfectly designed to handle that task. I have multiples in various places, and am considering getting a holster to keep mine close at hand.

Bobbins (spare): You'll want another bobbin for each color of thread you use frequently. Having spares around prevents you from needing to unwind a bobbin to put more thread of a different color on it. Bobbins shouldn't be wound with new thread on top of old—that can lead to poor balance and poor performance; always wind on an empty bobbin.

Marking chalk: This comes in all varieties, and I'd suggest having plenty of options on hand. I generally use my chalk cartridge, but I love my fine-tipped air erasable ink pen, and for fabrics with a deeper pile—like wools—I love my powdered wheel marking tool, which deposits powdered chalk using a toothed applicator that will actually make a mark in fluffier fabrics.

Clear acrylic ruler: This is one of the very few tools I have that I didn't grow up using, but really don't see how I'd get along without now. I have both a 3" × 18" (7.6cm × 45.7cm) and a 6" × 24" (15.2cm × 61cm) and they get plenty of exercise when I sew. Having a clear ruler that you can see through as you cut is invaluable for your accuracy, and it's an indispensable accompaniment for my rotary cutter.

Knitting needle: I use my knitting needles to turn straps inside out, to make points more pointy and to smooth out curves when I press. Such an inexpensive little gadget, and it's much better than most of the specialty gizmos that are on sale out there. Consider having multiples of various sizes for different tasks and fibers. And hey! You can even knit with them!

Pinking shears: If you're not using a serger (and most folks who are sewing at the intermediate level don't), you'll want to finish off your raw edges of your fabric in some way. You can overcast with your sewing machine, or you can pink the edges with pinking shears. In the clothing chapter, we'll talk a little more about other techniques, but I suspect that somewhere along the line you'll want to try your hand at these cool-looking shears.

Lots and lots of thread: I am the WORST at forgetting to purchase matching thread for my projects, but you really do need it. Beware of vintage threads—they have a shelf life, and if it breaks when you're using it in the machine, then it will break in your finished sewing, leaving you with a busted seam and a broken heart. Use newer, high-quality threads; the difference in price is pennies, but the difference in performance and satisfaction is huge. I never ever insist that sewing should cost a bunch of money—it really doesn't. But if I were to spend some cash, it would be on awesome shears and the best thread I can afford.

Pins and pin cushion: Get you some steel pins and a place to put them. I'm particularly partial to novelty pins, with little flowers on them. And I love the classic simplicity of a tomato pin cushion. While you might choose to use pins only for some seams but not for others, it is the rare stitcher indeed who has abandoned pins altogether in all situations. Pins are about confidence and accuracy, and you should use as many or as few as you deem necessary to get the results that please you.

Extra machine needles: You probably haven't been changing yours often enough. I have a suspicion that 80% of us (or more) don't change our needle as frequently as we should. Swap out for a new needle at the start of every new major project—which is to say, for each of the projects in this book. Yes, for each of them. You think it won't make a difference, but it really does—snarls disappear, stitches are more even, the machine glides through fabric more smoothly and you are suddenly having a much better time, all for less than a buck. Remember that needles come in sizes (bigger numbers equal fatter needles equal thicker fabrics), and some fibers (like knits and leather) have special needles just for them.

Organizer or sewing case: I use a plastic tackle box, which I keep open on my sewing table, as a catchall for my supplies. When you're first starting out with sewing, you might not need an organizer, but the more projects you do, the more leftover bits and pieces seem to accumulate, and you'll want to have a place to keep track of them (if only so you don't accidentally go out and buy them all over again when you already had three—ask me how I know). By keeping my kit right next to my machine, everything I need is right in reach as I sew.

Terminology and Techniques Review

With our tool kit all squared away and in order, a brief vocabulary lesson should get the cobwebs dusted off and ring some bells. Ringing bells make it easier to make music in the coming pages, people.

Backtacking: Also known as backstitching, this technique ties a "knot" at the beginning and end of each row of stitching. In order to prevent your seams from coming loose, you want them anchored, and I for one didn't pay all that money for a sewing machine so I could do them by hand. Instead, as you begin each seam, stitch forward two or three stitches and stop, reverse and stitch backward two or three stitches and stop, then continue the seam. Do the same as you finish each seam. Good girls backstitch every single seam; you do with that information what you choose.

Bias tape: These are strips of fabric cut on the bias, which is to say, diagonal to the grainline. These can be cut any width, one strip at a time or continuously. They're usually used to edge-finish quilts, but I use them frequently to bind seams and make piping. Bias tape can be made in single-fold or double-fold versions. Double-fold bias tape is single-fold bias tape that has been pressed again in half, right down the middle.

Clipping (corners and curves): Using your scissors, snip into a seam allowance up to the stitches but not through them. This allows you to release the seam allowance fabric, which will let outward curves avoid stretching and inward curves lie flat. Purists will tell you that notches are better than clips for outward curves, but I find that they weaken the seam, and prefer to snip regardless of whether a curve is concave or convex.

Curved seams: The partner to straight seams, these require a teensy bit more concentration but lend so much depth and complexity to projects that they're worth the extra time. Remember for all your seams to use the score marks on your sewing machine's throat plate to maintain a clean, consistent seam allowance.

Ease stitching: These are long, straight stitches that resemble gathering stitches but without all the volume. Used where you're connecting a larger piece to a smaller, such as a sleeve to an armhole opening, you draw up on ease stitches in order to reduce the length of a seamline so it will match an opposing seam better. Use your basting stitch here, same as for gathering.

Edgestitching: This is very similar to topstitching except it runs parallel to a garment or project edge, rather than a seam. Work to keep the distance from the edge to the stitches very consistent as you sew, since that's what people will notice the most.

Gathering stitches: Gathering takes a longer piece of fabric and shrinks down the length so it will match a shorter edge, resulting in small rounded tufts that are lovely and soft. There are multiple ways to create gathers, but the most common involves your basting stitch. Using your longest straight stitch, run a row of stitches along the seamline, then another in the seam allowance. Hold the bobbin thread firmly in your hand while moving the fabric along the threads like a curtain on a curtain rod. You've made gathers!

Grainline: Possibly the most important word when working with fabric, the grainline runs parallel to the selvage edge and represents the direction of the fabric's weave that has the most stability. Most all patterns will give you an indication of how a pattern piece should be laid out in relation to the grainline—pay attention and do as you're told! While it's not the end of the world to be off-grain, it really can make an impact on how nicely a garment hangs or whether or not a quilt becomes warped. You'll be happier with your results, and it only takes a second.

Hem: At the lower edge of a garment or project, you'll want to turn up the last bits of raw fabric edge and catch them in stitches. This is a hem, which should be pressed evenly and to a consistent depth prior to sewing in place. To most accurately place your pattern pieces on-grain, lay them out with the grainline indicator (usually an arrow) parallel to the selvage, then measure in from the selvage to the arrow along its length. Keeping that measurement equal makes the piece perfectly straight!

Clipping curves

Grainline, selvage, bias, crossgrain

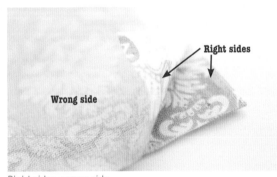

Right sides, wrong side

Topstitching

Press (versus ironing): Ironing involves a back-and-forth movement, designed to remove wrinkles. Pressing, on the other hand, involves a vertical movement, designed to remove bulk. In sewing, we press more than we iron, because our goal is to make the seams lie flat and fall the way we want. Press by placing the iron flat, allowing it to sit for five or six seconds, then lifting it and lowering again on a new section that overlaps the first.

Right sides and wrong sides: All fabric has a right side and a wrong side. For printed fabrics, it's usually pretty easy to spot; for solids and some apparel fabrics, it can be tougher. The answer when you don't know which is which is always to be consistent as you assemble your project—right and wrong, in this case, can be pretty subjective.

Selvage: This is the machine-made edge along the two sides of your fabric. Also called the selvage edge, it's usually about ⅝" (1.6cm) wide and has the nasty habit of shrinking at a different rate than the rest of your fabric. For that reason, your selvages ought to be removed before you sew, or cut around as you cut our your projects.

Straight-line stitching: This is just what it sounds like, and comprises some 85 percent of your sewing. Try as they might to make sewing seem like it's a complex mysterious process, at the end it's all just making stitches in straight lines or in curves. You can totally do that already! You're, like, more than halfway there!

Topstitching: This technique involves stitching a row parallel to an existing seam. It serves to anchor seam allowances in place, reinforce seams and create a slightly more casual, finished look to a project. Topstitching should be done with a slightly longer stitch length (about a 3 or 3.5 rather than the 2.5 you might normally use) and can be done with a heavier, thicker thread to make it really "pop."

Understitching: This technique is used to secure seam allowances to a lining from the inside, invisibly, and most often is called for when anchoring a lining or facing in place so it won't roll to the outside. Take care to prevent any bubbles as you stitch the seam allowances down, as those can make more bulk rather than the less that you're trying to achieve.

WARM-UP PROJECTS

Now that we're all on the same page as far as supplies and techniques, let's warm up a bit on some mini-projects that will get you back in gear and ready to party. I'm going into this book assuming that you have some sewing experience, but these projects ought to give you a solid idea of whether you're ready for the ones that come after. We're working on double-checking the straightness of seams, the consistency of seam allowances and your comfort level with the terms I'll be using in the rest of the book. I feel good about where you are now, but nobody ever regretted doing a lap before committing to a location, so let's tour your machine and flex your fingers.

Round Sachet With Herbs

This project can be as simple or as complicated as you like—add ribbon trim, ruffles, buttons and beads, almost anything you like if you want to jazz it up! I like it best in simple, beautiful fabrics (I often pull some from my scraps when I'm done working with fabrics I really, really love and want to see every day).

1. Use a glass or bowl to draw a circle. Trace this onto newsprint, printer paper or card stock. Cut two circles from cotton fabric.

2. Place the circles right sides together, then stitch around the curved edge using a ½" (1.3cm) seam allowance and leaving a 2" (5.1cm) opening unstitched.

3. Clip the curve around the entire seam allowance, up to but not through the stitching, to ease the seam allowance and permit you to turn the circle right-side out without any puckering or pulling.

4. Turn right-side out and press nice and smooth.

5. Fill with herbs like lavender, orange peel or rose petals. Topstitch around the outer edge, catching the opening shut as you do. Place in your dresser drawer with your undies or sweaters. Yum!

Small Drawstring Tote

This small and super-simple tote doesn't ask you to do anything you haven't done before, but it gives you a chance to think about construction and order of operations. Use ribbon, cord or a long strip of fabric folded in two for your drawstring.

1. Cut two rectangles of fabric measuring 10" × 6" (25.4cm × 15.2cm). Place right sides together and stitch a ½" (1.3cm) seam allowance down one long side, pivoting at the corner. Continue across the bottom edge, pivot again and stitch up the second long side. Leave the top edge unstitched.

2. Clip the corners at the bottom of the bag. Pink the edges of the seam allowances.

3. Press under the upper edge ¼" (6.4cm), then again another ¾" (1.9cm), taking care to keep the seam allowances open. Stitch around the entire upper edge, leaving an opening about 1" (2.5cm) wide unstitched.

4. Turn right-side out. Thread a drawstring through the opening and draw up the bag. Done!

Zippered Pencil Bag With Ruffles

Zippers—ah yes, those tricky but essential things. Use this handy, ruffly project to re-introduce yourself to zippers. Before you know it, they'll be your new best friends. And you'll have this awesome zip bag—great for storing pencils, notion or whatever strikes your ruffled fancy.

1. Cut two rectangles of fabric measuring 12" × 5" (30.5cm × 12.7cm) for the body of the bag. Cut three strips of fabric measuring 30" × 1" (76.2cm × 2.5cm) for the ruffles.

2. Place the two bag pieces right sides together and baste along the upper long edge where you want the zipper to be, using a ½" (1.3cm) seam allowance. Press seam allowances open.

3. Unzip the zipper and place face down on the wrong side of the seam. Line the right-hand zipper teeth up with the seam line. Holding the right leg of the zipper tape and the right seam allowance only, flip the right hand side of the bag out of the way so you can baste through the zipper tape and seam allowance, from top to bottom. You can find more detailed versions of these instructions in *Stitch by Stitch* or on the instruction card that comes with your zipper, under the heading "Centered Application."

4. Turn the whole puppy over. Place a strip of ½" (1.3cm) clear tape over the seam, as neatly and straight as you're able. Using the edges of the tape as a guide, topstitch through the fabric, the seam allowances and the zipper tape on both sides, from top to bottom.

5. Along the long edges on both sides of the long strips, stitch an overcast edge to prevent unraveling. Then stitch a gathering stitch down the center of each strip and draw them up until they measure 12" (30.5cm) long.

6. Place each strip on the right side of one of the 12" × 5" (30.5cm × 12.7cm) rectangles and stitch securely down the center, working to space them evenly below the zipper.

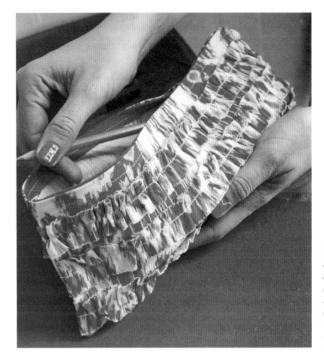

7. Slightly unzip the zipper. Fold the fabric so the two sides of the bag are right sides together. Stitch down one side, catching the tail end of the zipper tape, pivot at the corner, stitch across the lower edge, pivot again and sew up the third side. Clip the lower corners.

8. Turn right-side out and pat yourself on the back!

Now that you've warmed up yourself and your machine, let's boogie on over to the major projects! Feel free to begin wherever you choose, based on your interests and your goals for your own sewing—this is a super personalized passion, after all. Refer back to the **"How to Use This Book"** section on page 6 if you have questions, and remember: There are no mistakes in sewing, just times when you wish you'd done it a different way. You'll never know how until you try, so sharpen your needles and let those engines roar!

SECTION 1:
HOME DÉCOR

One of the most popular types of sewing, especially for those new to stitching but also for those who have been sewing for years and years, is sewing for the home. It's not just for the obvious reason that all of us have homes and want them to be beautiful; maybe more importantly, we all want our homes to look the way we feel, and to make us want to be there more often. The joy and excitement of welcoming someone into a room where you have designed and stitched every drape, pillow, slipcover and throw is really unparalleled. You'll never look at a bare room the same way again. Get ready to be drunk with power, people.

LEVEL 1 | RIBBONED ENVELOPE PILLOW

There are few things most folks like more than a nice pillow. I've written before about how deeply I dislike and distrust super-duper expensive pillows, especially since even at the astronomical prices I see in the stores, they're never quite what I want. This quick and clean pillow project is a great alternative to a zippered pillow and can be adapted to nearly any size or shape pillow insert. Instructions below are for a standard 16" × 16" (40.6cm × 40.6cm) pillow form. Should you select a different pillow form insert size, adjust your measurements accordingly—but isn't it nice to know that the skill is nearly universal?

SUPPLIES

½ yd (45.7 cm) fabric for body of the pillow (any weight)

5–6 yds (4.6-5.5 m) of 2" (5.1cm) ribbon for decorative trim

Matching thread

16" × 16" (40.6cm × 40.6cm) pillow form

Cut Fabric

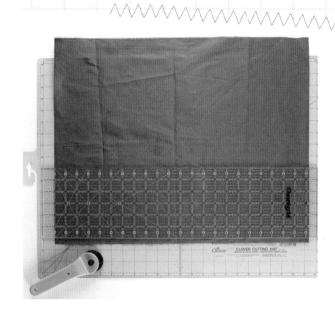

CUT

Cut one piece of fabric measuring 17" × 17" (43.2cm × 43.2cm) for the front of the pillow. Cut two pieces measuring 17" × 12.5" (43.2cm × 31.8cm) for the overlapping envelope back.

STANDARD PILLOW SIZES AND CUTTING MEASUREMENTS

Pillow size	Cutting size, front (cut one)	Cutting size, back (cut two)
12" × 12" (30.48cm × 30.48cm)	**13" × 13"** (33.02cm × 33.02cm)	**13" × 9.75"** (33.02cm × 24.77cm)
14" × 14" (35.56cm × 35.56cm)	**15" × 15"** (38.10cm × 38.10cm)	**15" ×11.25"** (38.10cm × 28.58cm)
16" × 16" (40.64cm × 40.64cm)	**17" × 17"** (43.18cm × 43.18cm)	**17" ×12.5"** (43.18cm × 31.75cm)
18" × 18" (45.72cm × 45.72cm)	**19" × 19"** (48.26cm × 48.26cm)	**19" × 14.25"** (48.26cm × 36.20cm)
20" × 20" (50.80cm × 50.80cm)	**21" × 21"** (53.34cm × 53.34cm)	**21" × 15.75"** (53.34cm × 40.01cm)
22" × 22" (55.88cm × 55.88cm)	**23" × 23"** (58.42cm × 58.42cm)	**23" × 17.25"** (58.42cm × 43.82cm)

Pillow Front and Envelope Back

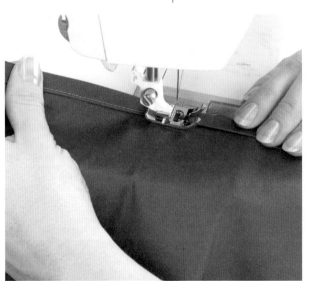

FOLD UNDER AND STITCH

On one long edge of each of the two back pieces, fold under and press ¼" (6.4mm), then fold under and press another ¼" (6.4mm). Stitch very close to the inner edge to create a narrow hem.

Create the Ribbon Effect

Using 2" (5.1cm) wide satin or sheer ribbon, create the ribbon detail on the pillow front. (You can also do this with grosgrain or Petersham ribbon, which I love; see the sidebar below for finer points of distinction.)

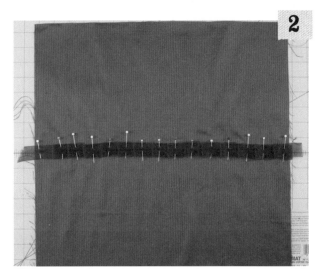

1. BEGIN PLEATING AND PINNING
Begin at the center of the pillow—you can mark the exact center by folding the pillow front in half and pressing lightly to make a crease. Center the length of ribbon over the creased line. Begin pleating ½" (1.3cm) away from the raw edge to leave room for the seam allowance, and keeping each pleat nice and evenly spaced.

2. PLEAT ACROSS PILLOW
Continue pleating all across the pillow front to the opposite side, again leaving ½" (1.3cm) unpleated at the raw edge.

GROSGRAIN VS. PETERSHAM RIBBON

The pillow here is made with sheer ribbon, but a pretty grosgrain would make a classic option. Grosgrain ribbon is familiar to most of us: the sweet ridged ribbon that adorns lots of children's things and is available in most fabric shops in various widths. Its close cousin, Petersham ribbon, is often mistaken for grosgrain, but they're really not the same ribbon. The easiest way to tell the difference is to look closely at the edges of the ribbon: Grosgrain has a straight edge, while Petersham is slightly scalloped. This is the result of the manufacturing process, and also makes grosgrain slightly stiffer than Petersham, which is a lovely ribbon that is both pliable and strong, making it a great choice for waistbands and ties on garments. There is no real qualitative difference between the two ribbons, no matter what anyone says; some projects call for stiffer ribbon, like grosgrain, and some call for drapier ribbon, like Petersham. You choose the look you prefer for your pillow—you're the designer, after all!

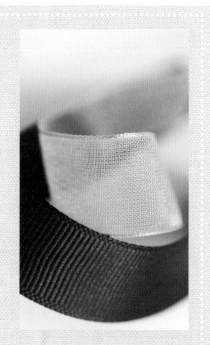

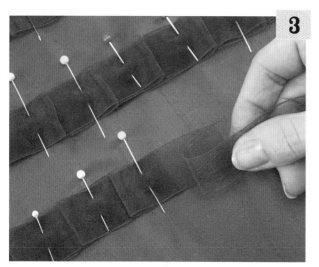

3. PLEAT ABOVE AND BELOW, REVERSING DIRECTION

Repeat above and below the center pleat, reversing the direction of the pleat with each row. Pin every individual pleat in place as you work. Pressing can help with stiffer ribbons, but test first! Ribbons with a high poly content are likely to melt at high heat.

4. STITCH PLEATS IN PLACE

When all pleats are pinned, sew a row of stitches down the center of each pleated row, always sewing in the direction of the pleats. Backtack at each end.

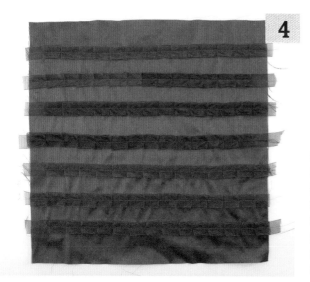

TRY THIS, TOO

There are about a zillion ways you can make this pillow that go beyond using the ribbon shown here! How about a simple envelope pillow, with no decoration at all? That's an excellent way to showcase a fabric you truly love, or one that has a little more going on—like a tapestry or textured fabric. Or how about using rickrack, that most useful of embellishments? Treat it just like the ribbon, either pleated or interlaced, and get ready to rock. Maybe you'd like to appliqué the front? Or make a patchwork panel for the front and an envelope back? Knock yourself out! What you'll find pretty quickly, especially with pillows, is that once you master the basic shapes, the sky's the limit.

Assemble the Pillow

1. PIN FRONT TO BACK PIECES

Once the pleating is complete, place the pillow front right-side up on your work surface. Lay one pillow back right sides together with the pillow front, then the other, taking care to overlap the hemmed edges and keep all other raw edges even. Pin around the outer edge to secure.

2. STITCH EDGES

Begin sewing the two edges that hold the overlapped panels. Sew all the way from one raw edge to the other, not stopping to pivot at the corners, and backtacking at each end.

Sew the other two edges in the same way as the first two, running your stitches right off each end.

3. TURN RIGHT-SIDE OUT

Clip corners at a diagonal. When you're finished, turn right-side out, pressing the edges of the pillow for a nice crisp look.

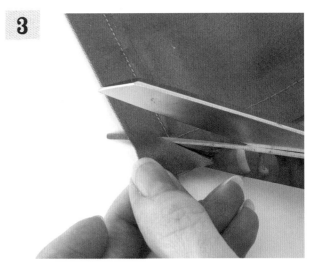

NEXT STEPS

Did you love making the pleats on the ribbon for this pillow? Try the **Sashiko Window Treatment** next (see page 42) and work on your box pleat skills!

The simple cutting and 90 degrees on this pillow will lead straight into the skills used in making the **Paving Stones Quilt** (see page 52), which is entirely made up of simple patchwork and straight lines.

For a lovely heirloom-quality bed set, pair this with the **Whole Cloth Quilt** (see page 84) and make your guest room a spa-like retreat.

LEVEL 2 | FOOTSTOOL SLIPCOVER WITH PIPING

With so much furniture out there at yard sales, flea markets and your mother's attic, it's almost crazy to buy new—especially once you learn to stitch a quick slipcover to transform it into something fabulous and stylish! Simple semi-fitted slipcovers are easy to make, and with only the most rudimentary of math, you can make a piece of old furniture look better than brand-new.

SUPPLIES

Footstool

Chart on enclosed CD

Measuring tape

Home dec weight cotton or linen fabric (yardage will vary based on the size of your furniture)

$\frac{6}{32}$" (4.8mm) of piping filler cord

2" (5.1cm) of single-fold bias tape to coordinate with your fabric

Matching thread

Prepare the Measurements

Maybe the most intimidating thing about making a slipcover, for most folks, is the measuring. The good news is that just a very few measurements and some nifty math tricks will help make this a ton easier and less scary. Let's start by getting out your tape measure—NOT your ruler. Your ruler is hard, and really is only good at measuring hard things, while your tape measure is soft and will take those curves and tufted bits and get you a really accurate number. Do note that a metal tape measure, like contractors use, is completely acceptable here (but not when you're making clothes, just FYI).

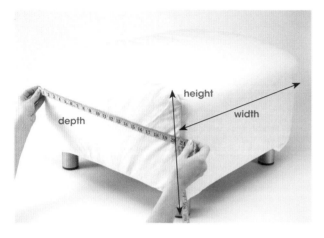

MEASURE FOOTSTOOL

Measure the height of your footstool, from floor to top. Next, measure the width, from west to east (side to side). Finally, measure the depth, from front to back. Note these in the chart you can print out from the CD enclosed.

Now you'll complete the chart to get your final measurements for the fabric, which you'll cut in the next section.

First, add seam allowances: You'll want ½" (1.3mm) seam allowance on each side, and since each of these pieces has two sides, you'll be adding an inch (2.5 cm) to each measurement you just took. Do that really hard math (tee-hee!) and make a note of the new numbers on the chart.

Finally, you'll want a little ease to allow you to get the slipcover on and off. Ease is that teeny extra bit of fabric that gives you some room to manipulate. No matter how perfect your measurements are, you'll want a little margin so your slipcover doesn't turn into a squeeze-cover. Add another inch—which gives you just ½" (1.3mm) on each side—to the measurements you have noted. Add it in the final, bold column on the chart.

That's it! You won't need a ton of other numbers for this version, so hang in there, kiddo.

Cut Fabric and Prepare the Piping

You'll use the handy-dandy chart you completed in the previous section as your guide for cutting out the fabric.

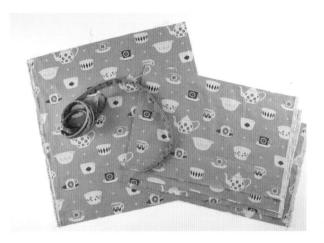

CUT PIECES

Begin by cutting the top of the slipcover. You'll use the width measurement and the depth measurement for this. For example, if my footstool is 24" (61cm) wide and 18" (45.7cm) deep, I want to cut a piece of my fabric that measures 26" × 20" (66cm × 50.8cm): (24 + 1 + 1) × (18 + 1 + 1). Keep in mind that the length for which you're measuring is the finished length, which might not necessarily be to the floor!

Next, cut four side pieces, using the width x height dimensions. For some footstools, you'll need two that are width x height and two that are depth x height—it all depends on whether your footstool is a cube or a rectangle. Use your eyeballs to figure it out—I know you can do it!

Assemble your piping (which is shown above) by making continuous bias tape (see page 10 for explanation as needed), then basting the bias tape around a length of piping filler cord (see the Crash Course below for a quick refresher on piping). I strongly recommend using fabric to cover your cording that is the same weight as the fabric you're using for your slipcover—you'll find that it wears longer and looks more cohesive that way.

CRASH COURSE: PIPING

Piping can be purchased pre-made, in little packages at the fabric shop, but I so prefer to make my own. It gives me so much more choice over my fabrics and control over the final product as I'm sewing!

1. COVER CORD

To make piping, purchase at least 6"(15.2cm) more length in piping filler cord than the seam you're planning to pipe—the extra length is for joining the piping ends together to make a neat finish. Then insert the cording into the center of the wrong side of a piece of bias tape. Bring the raw edges of the bias tape together, squeezing the piping in the center.

2. BASTE

Baste as close as possible to edge of piping filler cord using a zipper or piping foot. Remember: you want to keep the piping really super SNUG in order to make it pop on your final project! Trim the seam allowance down until it equals the seam allowance for your project, and you're good to go!

Stitch the Sides Together

Set the piece for the top of the footstool aside for now, and grab the four side pieces. Here you'll attach the sides, and in a later section, you'll attach this square "tube" of sides to the top after it is piped.

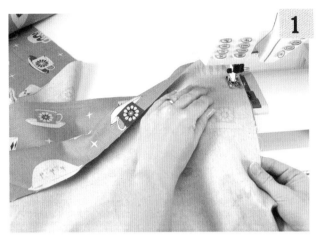

1. STITCH FOUR SIDES TOGETHER

Place one of the side pieces right sides together with the piece that goes next to it. Stitch a ½" (1.3cm) seam. Press your seam allowances open. Open out that pair, and add the next side piece, stitching it right sides together with its neighbor, using the same seam allowance. Continue until all four pieces are joined in a long strip (see Fig. 1 below).

2. JOIN THE ENDS

Take the strip of four panels and join them in a circle. Sew this fourth seam using the ½" (1.3cm) seam allowance, and then press open and set aside.

| LEFT SIDE | FRONT | RIGHT SIDE | BACK |

Fig. 1

Add the Piping

To add piping in the seams, we'll first baste it to the slipcover top, then join the top to the "tube" we made of the sides in the last section. To baste the piping to the slipcover top, you can either use your zipper foot or a presser foot specifically intended for piping—usually called a cording foot or a welting foot. Should you choose to use a cording foot, do keep in mind that they come in various sizes, and you'll want to use a cording foot that is as big as or bigger than the diameter of your piping. See more details in the sidebar on page 27.

1. PIN PIPING TO TOP

Pin the length of piping to all four edges of the top of the slipcover (which, at this point, is a piece on its own). Start in the center of one edge (not at a corner), and leave the first few inches (5.1cm) of piping unattached.

2. SNIP SEAM ALLOWANCE AT CORNERS

As you come to each corner, stop ½" (1.3cm) from the end and snip into the seam allowance of the piping only—not the slipcover top—up to the stitches but not through them; this allows you to turn a nice, crisp corner.

3. BASTE PIPING IN PLACE

Once the piping is pinned in place, stitch it down using basting stitches and your zipper or piping foot. Do this for each side as you add the piping. Rather than pinning all the way around, you'll pin one side, then baste, then remove the pins, then pin another side, then baste, and on, until you've basted all four sides. This makes for fewer mistakes, and allows you to baste straight off the edge at the end of each side, which will give you super crisp piping with no need to pivot.

4. OPEN STITCHES AT END AND PEEL BACK

When you get back to where you started, you want to mask the ends of the piping and create the illusion that there is a single piece of piping here. Trim the first end clean and flush so you're working with a neat tip. Then open up the opposite end by ripping out the basting stitches and peeling it like a banana.

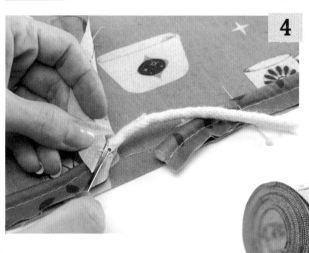

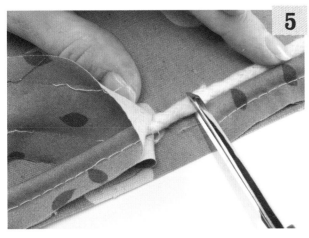

5. TRIM CORDING

Lay the two ends side by side, and trim just the cording—not the bias tape—on the second end so that the two pieces of cording butt up against one another and almost kiss (but in a nice way).

6. FOLD RAW EDGE AND PIN

Fold under the raw edge of the second end of the bias tape—because a folded edge is a finished edge!—and lay the first end inside it, right up against the second end.

7. FINISH BASTING

Wrap the bias tape back around and pin it in place. Finish basting the piping in place, catching the folded bit of bias tape and securing it as you do so.

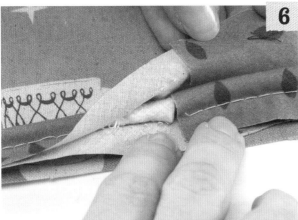

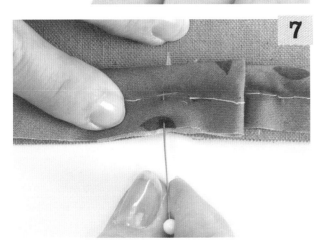

THE PIPING FOOT

Unlike a zipper foot, which is designed to allow the needle to get very close to the edge of the zipper teeth—and which can be used very successfully to stitch piping—a presser foot made specifically for piping has a tunnel beneath it into which the cording fits perfectly. Also called a cording foot, this means that rather than you having to manually smoosh the cording up against the edge of the zipper foot, the presser foot itself maintains control and places the needle much closer to the edge of the cording than you could do yourself. Be prepared to pay about twenty-five dollars, which might seem like a chunk of change, but if you're doing a lot of piping—like, all your sofa cushions, for example—it could very well be the best investment you make this year.

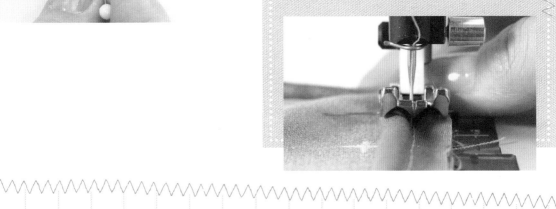

Assemble the Slipcover

1

1. PIN TOP TO SIDES

Place the piped slipcover top right-side up on your work surface. Take the "tube" made from the slipcover sides and begin matching it up to the slipcover top: Each seam at the corner of the tube should line up with a corner of the piped top. If it doesn't, NOW is the time to address that: too big, take out more seam allowance to make the tube smaller; too small, rip out your seams and use a smaller seam allowance. Pin each corner of the top to its matching seam to secure.

Once you have pinned the corners, continue pinning all the way around the edges to secure them prior to sewing. I find it super useful to place my pins through the cording itself so they don't poke out at an odd angle and stab me repeatedly in the fingers as I work.

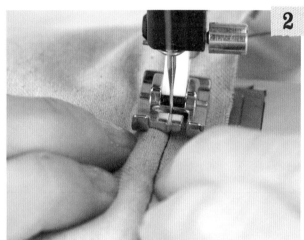

2

2. STITCH IN PLACE

Take the whole shebang to the sewing machine and, still with your piping or zipper foot, stitch it in place using your default, non-basting stitch length. At each corner, stitch all the way off the edge, then begin again on the next edge, with a whole new seam. This allows you to get a nice crisp corner so you'll be able to corner around that piping without running your needle through the cording and smooshing it flat unattractively.

Hem the Slipcover

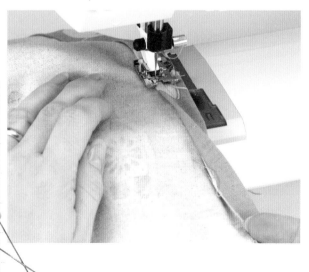

PRESS UNDER EDGES AND STITCH

Press under ½" (1.3cm) all the way around the lower edge of the slipcover. Press another ½" (1.3cm), then stitch all the way around. Consider using a decorative stitch or thread here if you want a little zing!

TRY THIS, TOO

Sometimes, a simple fitted slipcover just won't do. Sometimes, it's just gotta be a little more girly. I'm down with that—I have three girls, and they like a little fluffy now and then. To adapt this project for a gathered slipcover, just change the dimensions of the side panels!

For full gathers, increase the side-to-side measurement of each side panel by 1.5× its original dimension. For example, if my footstool is 15" (38.1cm) wide and 18" (45.7cm) tall, for the fitted slipcover I'd cut a side panel that's 17" × 20" (43.2cm × 50.8cm): (15 + 1 + 1 x 18 + 1 + 1). For a gathered one, I'd cut a panel that's 24½" × 20" (62.2cm × 50.8cm): (15 × 1.5 + 1 + 1 × 18 + 1 + 1). Which is to say, I don't have to adjust the height, because that hasn't changed; I only adjust the width to give me the extra fabric I need to make nice gathers.

Stitch the side panels together as above. Then, at the upper edge, run two rows of gathering stitches ½" (1.3cm) and ¼" (6.4mm) in from the raw edge. Draw up on those gathering stitches to reduce the length of the panels until they fit the piped top, then complete the assembly as you would for the fitted cover!

For an even fuller, fluffier slipcover, you can increase the width to 2× the original measurements, but keep in mind that fuller gathers don't always work well with stiffer fabrics. Doubling the length works great with lighter fabrics, like satins or even quilting cottons, but tends to fail when used with home décor fabrics.

NEXT STEPS

Nothing says warmth like a hot cup of tea. Move from this project to the **Tea Cozy** (see page 76) and work on a patchwork cover with some real heating power!

Love making cubes and adding piping to seams? Move on to the quilted **Sewing Machine Cover** (see page 64) and see how similar the two projects can be. Maybe you'll make your next slipcover with quilting!

Making clean, square corners can create shapes of all uses— turn your new skill to the **Fabric Picnic Basket** (see page 106) and see how a slipcover turned upside down can become a basket for all manner of goodies.

LEVEL 3 | TUFTED DUVET

I don't move my furniture around very often, and I almost never change the color of my walls (it took so long to choose the perfect paint color, I really don't want to do it again—and don't even get me started on the taping and the rollers), but what I do change frequently is the fabric that makes up a room. In my boudoir, specifically—and feel free to call yours a boudoir, too, it makes all the difference—I like to change the linens and colors from season to season to refresh my love for the space and to create a sanctuary that is meant only for me. A duvet is a quick, simple way to transform the emotion of a room, and it takes a lot less sewing than you might think. Combine fabric you love with a store-bought duvet insert for a project that will give your room a facelift in less time than it takes to tap dance.

SUPPLIES

Cotton or linen fabric
(yardage will vary—see
page 31)

Buttons to cover

Matching thread

Duvet (purchased
uncovered—I got mine at a
large retailer for very little)

Getting Started

I should point out here that we will be making a duvet cover, inserting a store-bought duvet into that cover and then stitching it closed. In other words, the duvet cover is not removable. So to please your desire for options, consider choosing a different fabric for each side. You'll stitch buttons on both sides, so it's totally reversible.

STANDARD COMFORTER/DUVET MEASUREMENTS

Crib: 36" × 60" (91.4cm × 152.4cm)
Twin: 66" × 88" (167.6cm × 223.5cm)
Full/Queen: 84" × 88"
(213.4cm × 223.5cm)
King: 88" × 106" (213.4cm × 269.2cm)

Keep in mind that these yardages are based on standard bed covering dimensions. Should you purchase a duvet from a big-box Swedish design store that has non-standard measurements, be sure to double-check that you'll have enough before cutting. Just divide your yards down into inches and compare to the length and width of the duvet you plan to cover.

1. CUT FABRIC TO SIZE

Cut your fabric to the following dimensions, depending on the size of your duvet (all measurements assume you'll be using 45" (114.3cm)-wide quilt-weight cotton; if your fabric is of a different width, adjust as necessary):
Crib: Two pieces 1⅜ yards (1.2 m) long
Twin: Two pieces 1⅝ yards (1.5 m) long
Full: Two pieces 2½ yards (2.3 m) long
Queen: Two pieces 2¾ yards (2.5 m) long
King: Two pieces 3 yards (5.5 m) long
Repeat for backing.

2. CUT ONE PIECE IN HALF

Take one cut of fabric and set it aside. Divide the other cut of fabric in half down the center, longways, so that the length of the resulting two pieces is the same as before but they are half the width. Repeat with backing fabric.

OVERHANG AND DRAPE: AN ANALYSIS

When you look at the list of "standard" measurements for comforters, what you don't see is the amount of DROP included in that measurement. Simply put, drop is the amount of overhang beyond the edge of the mattress that a comforter or bedspread provides. Now, traditionally, the words *comforter* and *bedspread* actually allowed us to distinguish between a shorter and a longer drop: While most of us use them interchangeably, a comforter is actually a bed covering that has less drop, while a bedspread generally goes to or near the floor. For the purposes of this project, a duvet is considered a comforter; should you want a longer drop, you'll need more fabric to ensure that your cover goes all the way to the floor—along with batting to fill it, as most store-bought duvets are of the short-drop variety.

Assemble the Duvet

For a bed covering or curtain, having a seam right up the center of the piece is distracting and has the unfortunate effect of looking haphazard and unplanned. Instead, we want to offset the seams so they're on either side of the center, giving them the appearance of being part of the overall design. That explains why you cut one of the lengths of fabric in half lengthwise: so we can deliberately place our seams to give design cohesiveness to the duvet. Did you know you were so cool? I'm totally calling you a "designer" from now on.

FIG. 1

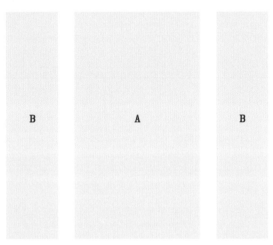

1. STITCH SIDE PANELS TO CENTER PANEL

First, remove the selvages from all pieces. Lay the center (uncut) panel right-side up on a smooth work surface. Place one of the two narrow side panels right sides together and raw edges even with one long edge of the center panel. Pin in place and stitch using a ½" (1.3cm) seam allowance. Press seam allowances open. Repeat with other side panel. Fig. 1 shows how the panels are assembled.

Repeat step 1 with the backing fabric.

Consider ironing it brutally prior to this step. It's a lot of fabric, and your work will be easier if it has been steamed into submission first.

2. PIN FRONT TO BACK AND CHECK SIZE

Place the front of the duvet on the work surface, right-side up. Place the backing right sides together with the front. Align all raw edges. Measure and mark the finished size of your duvet plus seam allowances: Crib (38" × 62" [96.5 cm × 157.5 cm]); Twin (68" × 90" [172.7 cm × 228.6 cm]); Full/Queen (86" × 90" [218.4 cm × 228.6 cm]); King (92" × 110" [233.7 cm × 279.4 cm]). (Note: You might need to leave on the selvages to make 90" (228.6 cm) width on the king size.) You'll find that your front and backing are slightly larger than these measurements. With the center panel still centered, trim the edges down until they are the correct size for your chosen duvet.

3. STITCH FRONT AND BACK TOGETHER

Pin these newly cut edges together, and stitch a ½" (1.3cm) seam allowance all the way around the cover, pivoting at each corner, and leaving a 6"–8" (15.2 cm–20.3 cm) wide opening to turn.

4. TURN RIGHT SIDE OUT

Clip corners at a 45-degree angle. Flip right side out, using a knitting needle to really get a nice, sharp corner. Press all edges.

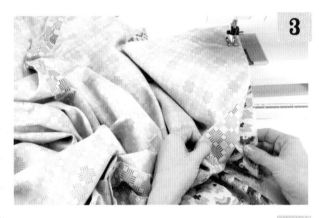

Tuft and Finish the Duvet

1. INSERT DUVET INTO COVER

Into the cover you've just sewn, insert the store-bought duvet. (If you'd prefer not to use a store-bought duvet, insert a layer of batting equal to the dimensions of your cover.)

2. MARK PLACE FOR TUFTS

Lay out the whole shootin' match and smooth to the edges, making sure all the filling is evenly distributed and situated where you want it. Once you tuft, it will all be secured in place, so you want to be careful that it's where you like it at this stage.

Starting at the center, mark where you want the tuffing to fall. I would suggest that you keep your tufts no more than 12" (30.5cm) from one another on all sides.

CRASH COURSE: COVERING BUTTONS

Buttons to cover come in lovely little kits that include a mold, a presser and aluminum button shapes. Use a small scrap of fabric large enough to go over the entire button shape. Keep these instructions in mind whenever a project calls for fun buttons.

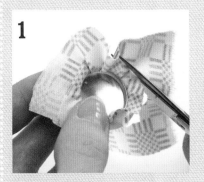

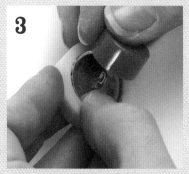

1. Place the fabric right-side down on top of the button mold. Place the button shank on top (but not actually on). You just want to see how much extra fabric needs to be trimmed. Trim the edges a bit.

2. Remove the shank and fold the edges into the mold. Place the button shank, shank facing out, into the mold.

3. Use the presser to push the shank into the mold until it snaps into place and anchors the fabric with it. Easy!

If you choose to make your duvet one-sided, it will need buttons only on the top. Complete all the steps below, but omit the part in step 5 where you pick up a second button. (But really, why wouldn't you want it reversible for the same amount of work?)

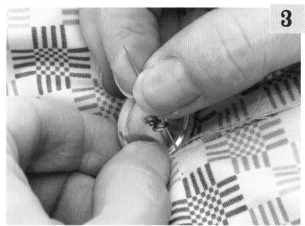

3. STITCH ON TOP BUTTON

Grab your extra-large covered buttons (see the Crash Course on the previous page, as needed), and beginning at the center of the duvet, place one on top of the mark you made in the previous step. With a threaded hand needle, sew from the underside to the mark on top; place the button on the needle and secure it to the duvet, creating a tuft as you do.

4. BRING NEEDLE BACK DOWN

Bring the needle back down through the duvet right next to the hole you first made.

5. STITCH BUTTON ON REVERSE

On the reverse side, pick up a second button and continue to sew as you did the other button.

6. SECURE BUTTONS

Stitch through the buttons three or more times to make them nice and snug, then tie off the thread. Repeat until all marks have been tufted.

7. TOPSTITCH

Topstitch around the entire edge of the duvet, catching the opening closed as you do. You'll be stitching through not just the layers of the duvet cover, but also of the duvet body here—that's what keeps the duvet in place so there isn't any scrunching or shifting later.

STITCH TIP

After you topstitch the duvet closed, consider stitching a second row, ¼" (6.4mm) inside the first, for a really professional look.

NEXT STEPS

Love the fluffy texture and loft of the duvet? Head over to the trapunto **Improvisational Landscape Wall Quilt** (see page 90) and learn techniques to make your sewing more three-dimensional.

Duvets are a clean, simple way to change your room décor easily. For something with more staying power and a different type of impact, introduce yourself to the **Whole Cloth Quilt** (see page 84)—it's almost certain to be an heirloom for many years (and generations) to come.

Adding covered buttons can become an obsession, and it doesn't take long to realize you can totally add them anywhere. Try making the **Wherever Jacket** (see page 206) with some covered buttons for a sleek look.

LEVEL 4 | PHOTO-TRANSFER WALL ART

Working with photos and fabric is a natural combination for a lot of people, since many of us began sewing because we have treasured memories of family members who sewed before us. Adding a photo of a family member increases the value of a piece of sewing for us later, and can be an incredibly touching gift to share. The steps are straightforward, but there is a learning curve here if you're new to photo-editing software or art quilting, so be willing to take your time and feel your way through the techniques—the results are completely worth it.

SUPPLIES

Photo to duplicate

PFD cotton or solution to soak printable fabric

Freezer paper

Found objects to embellish

Wood canvas stretchers

Wood glue

Staple gun

Prepare and Print the Photo

You'll need to choose an image you want to build around. You can use any image you want: your first house, your baby's first smile, your wedding day, a view from the window in the house where you grew up, a cool artsy photograph that you just love, absolutely anything.

Using freezer paper, we'll fuse fabric to a stiff surface that will allow us to send it right through our inkjet printer. It's worth pointing out that laser printers won't work for this, and certain inkjet printers have better long-term inks than others. Epson printers are very reliable, and HP are if you're using their Vivera inks.

Printing on a white or cream background fabric will create colors that are more or less true to the original image; keep in mind, though, that these are inks over other inks when you print on a colored fabric, and the colors might change when the two shades meet. This can create some really cool unexpected results, so don't shy away from it, but be prepared that your image might not be an exact duplicate of the photo.

1. EDIT PHOTO USING SOFTWARE

Pull your digital photo into your photo editing software (such as Adobe Photoshop Elements or Picasa).

Decrease the saturation of the colors or make the photo black and white or sepia. Use the software to enhance the light and dark sections of the photo to make them really pop.

Determine the finished size of your artwork. In the sample, I wanted a larger piece that measured about 16" × 21" (40.6cm × 53.3cm). Resize your image to meet those dimensions.

Since the image is larger than a single sheet, we'll need to print it on multiple sheets and then reconnect them (16" × 21" [40.6cm × 53.3cm] amounts to four 8.5" × 11" [21.6cm × 27.9cm] sheets of paper). Tile the image to print on multiple sheets. Set the margins of the pages to print overlapped by ½" (1.3cm) so you don't lose any of the image.

2. FUSE FREEZER PAPER TO FABRIC

Fuse large pieces of freezer paper to the wrong side of the fabric. Make sure it is stuck together. Then trim each fused sheet to very slightly below 8.5" × 11" (21.6cm × 27.9cm), making sure you've trimmed off any stray threads and snags that might gum up your printer.

3. PRINT PHOTO SHEETS

Adjust your printer to the "heavy paper" setting, and if you're able to increase the ink flow (usually by telling it "best quality" printing), then do that. Print the tiled image, which should come out on multiple sheets—a test print on regular paper isn't a bad idea here.

Piece the Sheets
With the image printed on multiple pages, we'll need to stitch it back together—literally.

1. ARRANGE PAGES AND TRIM
Arrange the pages so the photo is complete. Edges will overlap so the image appears to be seamless. Trim the edges that overlap–be sure just to trim only the edge that is on top. (Also see Fig. 1.)

2. STITCH FIRST ROW TOGETHER
Stitch your first row of sheets together. (I have three, but you might have two or four or five, depending on the size of your finished piece.) Stitch the sheets together ¼" (6.4mm) inside the edge with a straight stitch. Keep in mind that rather than sewing right sides together, you will sew with both sheets facing right-side up, with one edge overlapping the other.

3. STITCH PARALLEL SEAM
Then sew another seam parallel to it, about ¼" (6.4mm) away.
    Repeat steps 2-3 for the remaining rows of sheets.

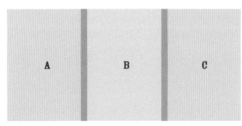

Fig. 1
Overlap right side of A over B. Overlap right side of B over C. Green areas indicate where edges overlap. Trim green edge on A. Trim green edge on B.

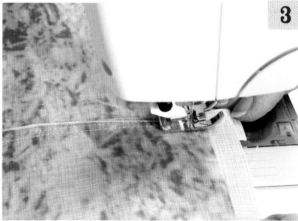

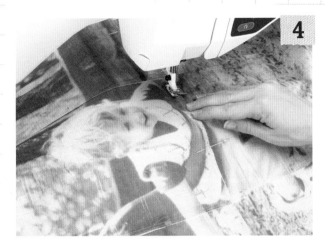

4. ATTACH ROWS TO ONE ANOTHER

Repeat steps 2–3 to attach the row together.

Peel off the freezer paper from the back of each sheet (save it, too, because it can totally be reused). Square up the fabric.

STITCH TIP

As you'll see, this method of stitching the overlapping rows will leave raw edges exposed. This lends texture to your finished wall art. But if you totally can't stand the rawness of this method, you can still have smooth seams. Turn under the raw edges of each abutting sheet ¼" (6.4mm) and slipstitch in place.

Add the Border

To attach your fabric to canvas stretchers, you'll need, from a local art supply store, to get a set of four canvas stretchers, which can be purchased in standard measurements. You'll want two "length" pieces and two "width" pieces, but the length and width don't have to be the same size. For example, I used 24" (61cm) for the "length" and 16" (40.6cm) for the "width" and purchased two of each of those sizes. Canvas stretchers are usually very affordable—in the two to four dollar range—and are super simple to assemble.

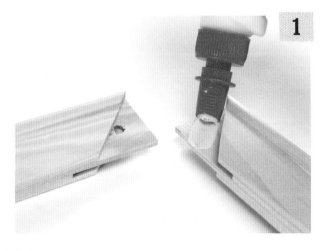

1. ASSEMBLE STRETCHER

There are divots and flanges on each end of the stretcher bars, and they're designed to work together. Spread a thin layer of wood glue on each side of the flange, and then insert it into the divot on the matching bar to form a 90-degree corner. Continue all the way around, until on the final stretcher bar you insert BOTH ends at the same time. Square up the frame, wipe away excess glue and leave it to dry for at least a couple of hours before adding your art.

The fabrics you choose for the border can be solid, prints or patchwork panels (see the quilting chapter for some patchwork ideas!). I love to use linen fabrics for this step, and give a subtle chic-but-old-fashioned three-dimensionality to the photo. More than one fabric can be added in borders that extend outward.

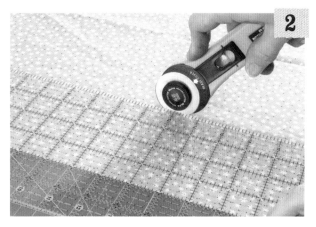

2. CUT FABRIC STRIPS

Cut four 4" (10.2cm) strips for the border. For length, use the width of the image or at least four inches longer than the longest side of your image; stitch shorter strips together, if necessary

3. MARK BORDER

Lay your image over the frame you've glued and mark where the border will intersect with the frame. The idea here is that we want to ensure that the image is smaller than the frame so that some of the border will be visible. Mark approximately 1½"–2" (3.8cm–5.1cm) inside the inner edge of the frame to indicate where you'll add the border.

4. STITCH BORDER TO IMAGE

Add the border on each of the four sides of the image, using the marks you've made as a guide.

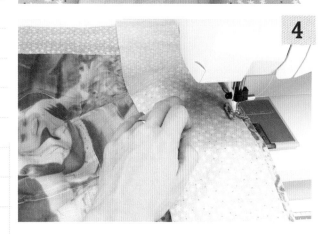

TRY THIS, TOO!

With the fabric and patchwork quality of this piece, you could turn it into a blanket or quilt. Check out the quilting chapter (starting on page 48) to learn how to back, bind and quilt a quilt. You could also make it the front of a pillow.

If you do make a quilt or pillow—and thus, plan on washing this thing—you will want to protect it. To ensure durability, use PFD muslin rather than regular fabric—PFD stands for "prepared for dye," and means the fabric is ready to absorb your inks better than another fabric might be. Alternately, you can soak the fabric in a solution marketed to prep fabric for inkjet printing, which can be found at many independent fabric shops or around the Web.

5. PREPARE TO ATTACH TO FRAME

With your border added and all the seams pressed nice and crisp, prepare to attach the image to the frame using a simple staple gun. With the image right-side down on your work surface, center it in the frame opening. Fold each corner back to make a triangle, then fold the edges to the back of the frame, making a mitered corner. Staple along one edge, about 2″ (5.1cm) apart.

6. STAPLE TO FRAME

Pull the opposite corner, then staple that, stretching the fabric just slightly as you do. Continue to staple around the back of the frame, working on opposite sides as you go to make sure you don't skew the image. Trim any excess fabric.

If you find wrinkles, bulges, or are unhappy, just take out the staples and try again! Do take care, though: After a while, you will have traumatized the edge of the fabric so much that you won't get another chance.

NEXT STEPS

Quilting and sewing offer opportunities to really break out of the expected and try things with fabric and thread that you might not have thought of previously. After making this framed piece of art, skip over to the **Improvisational Landscape Wall Quilt** (see page 90) and try your talents at a bit of art quilting!

The **Paving Stones Quilt** (see page 52) is a classic quilt pattern that invites you to work through a series of blocks that share a great deal in common with the layout of this art piece. Making a quilt can be every bit as artistic as working with a photographic image—and is a great next step!

Simple can be huge, no matter how it gets used. If memories matter to you, whip up the **Travel Matching Game** (see page 144) and build some new ones—then, years from now, you'll have one more photo to sew for your walls.

LEVEL 5 | SASHIKO WINDOW TREATMENT

There is something both luxurious and humble about linen that makes it a lovely candidate for a window treatment. Add Sashiko embroidery to the mix, and it becomes a chic statement of your endless good taste. Both the curtain and the embroidery look fancy, but can be completed with only the most basic tools and beginner-level skills—not that anyone needs to know that but you. Hang these using the rod pocket or with drapery clips.

SUPPLIES

Mid-weight linen (a piece that measures your desired curtain length plus 4" (10.2cm) by three times the desired finished width)

Sashiko thread in a contrasting color

Sashiko needles (these are like embroidery needles, but it's worth it to spring for the real thing)

Matching all-purpose sewing thread

Cut Fabric

I might humbly suggest using two of these curtains to cover a window (and I like mine to pool a bit on the ground, but that's up to you). Most of your nicer linens come in 60" (152.4cm) widths, and most windows are less than 40" (101.6cm) wide, so two curtains measuring 20" (50.8cm) will probably be plenty. If you haven't already, cut the fabric to size as indicated in the supplies list.

RIPPING RATHER THAN CUTTING

When cutting long pieces of fabric, keeping your edges straight can be nerve-racking. Simple solution: rip instead! Take a small snip into the edge of the fabric, then tear—you'll find that the fabric rips along a single thread, giving you a nice, straight line every time. Do be aware that this can traumatize the fabric a bit, giving it frayed edges like in these step-by-step photos, so if you've got some wiggle room, consider adding an extra ¼" (6.4mm) to your measurements to allow for that.

Make the Pleats

1. PRESS UNDER LONG EDGES

Press under the two long edges of the panel ¼" (6.4mm). Leave them be for now—we'll come back to them. At the upper edge, fold over ½" (1.3cm) and press securely. Baste in place—I know, no one likes to baste, but your life will be so much simpler if you take my advice. Trust me.

2. MARK LINES FOR PLEATS

Beginning at the long edge that will be centered on the window—called the leading edge, because it's the one that will draw the curtain when it is opened or closed—measure 3" (7.6cm) from the edge; using your marking pen or chalk, make a mark 5" (12.7cm) long from top to bottom on the wrong side of the fabric. Repeat every 3" (7.6cm) across the body of the panel, marking each time.

3. FOLD FABRIC AND PIN

With the fabric right sides together, fold the fabric so the first two marks on the leading edge touch one another. Pin in place.

Continue matching up the marks and pinning all the way across the panel until you reach the other side. Should you have a mark with no mate, leave it unpinned; this will fall at the side edge—which is to say, the edge of the curtain at the side of the window.

4. STITCH ALONG LINES

On the wrong side, stitch a seam from top to bottom of the 5" (12.7cm)-long marks you made. Backstitch at each end. Continue with the rest of the marks.

5. PRESS FOLDS FLAT

On the wrong side of the panel, take each fold made by the seams you've stitched vertically and smoosh it flat so that the center of the fold lies on top of the seam. Press in place, then repeat across the upper edge of the panel, pinning each pleat to secure.

6. BASTE PLEATS IN PLACE

Baste all those pleats in place. Sew all those pleats in place, using a ½" (1.3cm) seam allowance from the upper, pressed edge of the curtain. These stitches will show later, but if you'd prefer they didn't, you can baste here with your longest straight stitch and then hand-sew in a few steps.

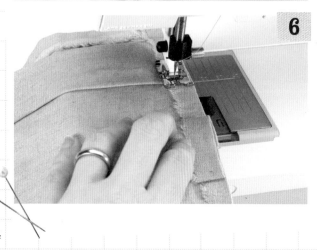

Install the Rod Pocket

1. CUT ROD POCKET AND PRESS EDGES

Cut a rectangle of fabric for the rod pocket measuring 6" (15.2cm) in height by the current width of the panel. Press under ¾" (1cm) on each of the long edges.

2. STITCH TO CURTAIN, LEAVING OPENING

Place the rod pocket panel right sides together with the curtain. At the sides of the curtain, where the edges have been pressed under, stitch a ½" (1.3cm) seam from bottom to top of the rod pocket BUT leave a small opening for your rod to slide through. (This can be pretty much anywhere, but I like to center mine so there is a small flange at the upper edge of the curtain, above the rod.) Be sure to backtack at the edges of the opening—your seam will look like this: backstitch; sew; backstitch; skip for the rod opening; backstitch; sew; backstitch at end of seam. Repeat on the other side.

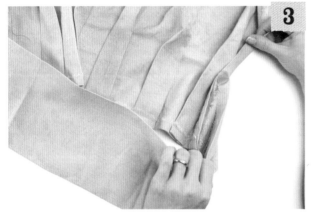

3. FLIP ROD POCKET

Flip the rod pocket to the wrong side of the curtain. As you do, you'll find the pressed-under edges turn themselves naturally to create a clean folded edge, just aching to be neatly hemmed. Cool trick, huh?

4. STITCH LOWER EDGE OF ROD POCKET

At the lower edge of the rod pocket, with the public side of your curtain down toward the machine, stitch ½" (1.3cm) away from the pressed edge from one side to the other, securing the rod pocket in place. Note: These stitches will be visible from the public side of the curtain, but if you'd rather they be masked, check out the hand-stitching instructions in the sidebar below.

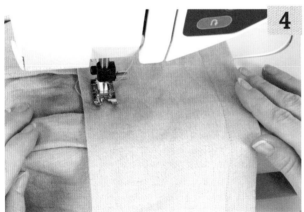

HANDSTITCHING FOR INVISIBLE SEAMS

For a super schmancy finish, you can use a slipstitch or whipstitch to sew the rod pocket in place rather than seam stitching. This ensures that no seam will show on the right side to mar the prettiness of your box pleats. Check out the possibilities on page 122.

Hem With Mitered Corners

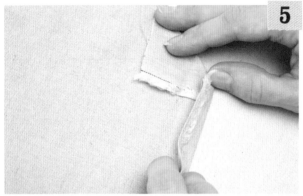

5. FOLD UP ¼" (6.4MM)

Fold up one lower corner at a 45-ish degree angle. At the bottom edge of the curtain panel, turn under ¼" (6.4mm) and press.

6. FOLD ANOTHER 3" (7.6CM)

Turn under another 3" (7.6cm) and press. Press well so that you will be able to see the creases. Then, open out the pressed fold.

7. TRIM TRIANGLE AND RE-FOLD

Because the side edge popped under when you made the rod pocket, it's all ready to be pressed in place. Then, trim out the point of the triangle you folded in to start with, then fold the pressed edges back in place. You should now have a clean edge down the side, across the lower edge of the curtain and up the other side.

8. STITCH EDGES

With the corners mitered, stitch down one long edge, catching the side hem, pivot at the lower corner, stitch across the lower hem, pivot again and stitch up the final long edge, taking care to begin and end below the stitches securing the rod pocket—won't get much curtain hanging done if that's sewn shut!

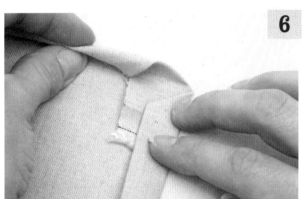

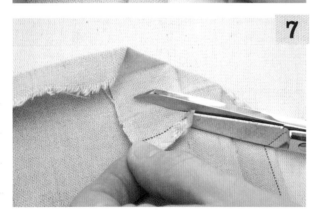

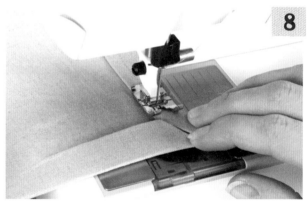

Adding the Sashiko embroidery is next, and it's really what makes these curtains. But if embroidery is not your thing, or perhaps you've chosen a fussy fabric design, these panels can certainly can be hung as they are, with no embroidery. If that's the case, you're done!

Add the Sashiko Embroidery

Sashiko—Japanese-style embroidery—designs tend to incorporate regular, repeated geometric motifs on a small scale. You can use a traditional design (the interlocking circles I went with are a common design), or create your own. Traditionally, Sashiko is sewn starting with the horizontal and vertical lines, then the diagonal lines, then any other designs are filled in.

1. TRANSFER DESIGN AND THREAD NEEDLE

Before you stitch, trace the embroidery design from paper to the curtain using a pen. If you have one available, a light box is a great way to do this, but if you don't, tape your fabric to a sunny window.

Next, thread a Sashiko needle with Sashiko thread, which is used whole rather than being divided into strands. You should have enough thread on your needle to complete one row of embroidery (so you can avoid knots in the back). While not essential, placing your curtain in an embroidery hoop can help keep your stitches more even.

2. STITCH VERTICAL ELEMENTS

Begin with the vertical elements by pulling the thread all the way through from the back and allowing the knot to rest on the wrong side of the fabric. Using the tip of the needle, move in and out of the fabric, collecting stitches on the needle as you do. Usually, you'll see half as much thread above the fabric as below, which is to say, the spaces between the stitches on the right side are slightly shorter than the stitches themselves. Once your needle is full, draw the thread through, again taking care not to pucker the fabric. When you complete the first line, cut the thread and tie a knot.

Begin the next line of stitching, but sew in the opposite direction—this will work to keep the fabric lying flat and smooth as you go, and avoid any stretching or warping of the weave.

3. COMPLETE HORIZONTAL STITCHES

Once all the vertical lines are complete, begin the horizontal lines in the same manner as step 3. (Keep in mind that if you choose a different design than the one on the CD, you'll need to complete the diagonal lines and then the remaining designs.)

NEXT STEPS

There's something so elegant about the clean box pleats in this window treatment—they're timeless and classy. Check out how they translate to clothing when you sew the **A-Line Skirt With Peek-a-Boo Pleat** (see page 180).

Sashiko embroidery is simple yet powerful, I wouldn't blame you for wanting to add it to everything. How about dressing up the **Everyday Shoulder Bag** (see page 100)?

SECTION 2:
PATCHWORK AND QUILTING

There has been a remarkable growth in the quilting world the past five years, and most of it is fueled by younger quilters with a more modern, streamlined design sense joining the craft. The art of using small cuts of fabric to create large-scale textile designs has evolved to include brighter colors, more inventive shapes, modern design sense and adventurous combinations. The projects that follow in this section introduce you to the modern quilting movement through all the basic skills, and give you the chance to consider piecing fabrics together to create a sum greater than its parts.

QUILTING BASICS

Some details about quilting are nearly universal in patchwork projects and patterns, so it's best to establish those ground rules right away. Mostly, I'm talking about the ¼" (6.4mm) presser foot and the ¼" (6.4mm) seam allowance, plus rotary cutting basics and a bit of pressing technique.

The ¼" (6.4mm) Presser Foot

Unlike your standard presser foot, which on most machines includes an oblong opening to allow your needle to go either forward or side to side (as in a zigzag stitch), a ¼" (6.4mm) presser foot allows for only forward movement. This is because this particular foot is uniquely designed to be used for stitching narrow seams on patchwork. The edge of the presser foot is set at ¼" (6.4mm) away from the needle, much closer to the needle than the edge of a standard presser foot, which is generally ⅜"–½" (9.5mm–1.3cm) away. Also called a patchwork foot or a piecework foot, the ¼" (6.4mm) foot is often sold as an accessory, and may not have come standard with your machine. They can usually be purchased for around twenty dollars.

Why bother with ¼" (6.4mm) seam allowances, though? Boy, am I glad you asked . . .

Checking Your ¼" (6.4mm) Seam Allowance

The heart of most modern quilting is the ¼" (6.4mm) seam allowance. Quilting tends to use much more scant seam allowances than, say, garment sewing because it permits the use of less fabric for each finished project. Since quilting has evolved from a tradition of scraps, using a smaller seam allowance makes total sense. You'll want to be sure that you're getting a good, accurate seam allowance, though, before you begin, so you can be certain that your results will be pleasing. This is less about slavish accuracy than it is about avoiding frustration in the future: If you make a series of quilt blocks that are all designed to fit together, and some are larger than others, then you're swimming in a pool of headache. So much better to work out this detail early on, so you'll love every second of the quilting you'll be doing going forward. Because make no mistake: It's far more addictive than it appears.

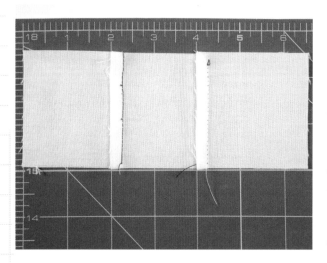

To check your seam allowance, cut three squares of fabric that each measure 2½" × 2½" (6.4cm × 6.4cm). Line them up, edge to edge.

Place the square on the left, right sides together, with the center square. Stitch a ¼" (6.4mm) seam along one edge. Open the two out, then place the square on the right, right sides together, along the opposite edge of the center square. Stitch another ¼" (6.4mm) seam allowance. Take the whole thing to the ironing board and press those seam allowances open. You should find that you have a piece that measures 6½" (16.5cm) across the long edge—if you do, then your ¼" (6.4mm) seam allowance is totally accurate! If not, press again and see if that does the trick. Alternately, adjust your presser foot or continue experimenting by moving your fabric just to the inside or just to the outside of that presser foot edge until you get an accurate ¼" (6.4mm) each time.

Cutting it Right

As you're checking these seam allowances, naturally you're doing math to see if they add up correctly. If you didn't cut your fabric well to begin with, though, all the adding in the world won't ever prove that you've got the right seam allowance. For better cutting, consider using a rotary cutter and mat.

A rotary cutter is basically a razor blade on a wheel. (Because it's so sharp, it has a safety, which should always be kept on when you aren't actively cutting.) Rotary cutters, because they're so sharp, can cut multiple layers of fabric at the same time, which is a lifesaver for quilters who tend to cut many pieces to the same dimensions—cutting through multiple layers greatly reduces the time necessary to cut out all those pieces.

With such a sharp blade, though, any surface on which you cut will be damaged by the blade unless there is a self-healing mat beneath it. The great advantage of the cutting mat is that it's marked with a grid in 1" (2.5cm) increments, allowing you to square up any piece of fabric you're cutting at the same time you're getting a nice straight cut. Here's how to do it right:

Place your fabric so it overlaps any vertical line. Trim off the edge using a clear acrylic ruler laid directly on top of and parallel to that vertical line. (Always move the rotary cutter away from you, never toward, for safety.) Use your non-dominant hand to hold the ruler nice and steady as you cut; move your hand gradually up the ruler, like a spider, as you cut. Once that first cut is good and straight, you can rotate your fabric 90 degrees, line the first cut edge up with any horizontal line, then repeat with a second cut along the vertical, making a perfect 90-degree corner!

On Pressing Seams

Most of us are accustomed to pressing our seams open. When you're working with ¼" (6.4mm) seam allowances, though, it can be tough to get those teeny bits of fabric to press apart without singeing your fingers. The advantage of pressing apart is that it allows you to get more accuracy in your measurements—you lose fewer fractions of inches to pressing errors, and those can add up—and it makes for a flatter seamline. Before you go assuming that pressing open is the clear way to go, consider that by pressing your seams to one side, especially when you're working with light fabrics stitched to dark fabrics, you're better able to prevent darker colors from "bleeding through" lighter ones when a dark fabric's seam allowance is behind a lighter fabric, making it visible from the front. In that case, pressing to the side, in the direction of the darker fabric, is a great way to go. Additionally, if you plan to quilt your patchwork in straight lines parallel to the seams, pressing your seam allowances to one side makes those stitches "pop" just a bit more.

In practice, most folks tend to choose pressing open or pressing to the side and doing that pretty much habitually. On occasion, I'll choose one or the other based on how I plan to work with the patchwork when it's done. Those kinds of questions are hard to anticipate, though, when you've never made a quilt before. So for now, let's just assume that you'll press to the side unless instructed otherwise.

The best way to figure out how to make all this information work for you is to get busy doing some actual patchwork. You ready? Let's quilt, y'all.

LEVEL 1 | PAVING STONES QUILT

What's that, didn't expect to make a whole quilt right at the very beginning? What better way to learn the steps and skills required to do the more complicated patchwork projects that follow? This modern design is based on simple principles, goes together quickly and is delightfully different every single time you stitch it up. Inspired by those paving stones you can buy at home improvement stores, the ones that have smaller tiles embossed inside them so that when you rotate the paving stone it looks like a new configuration of tiles each time, the single block that makes up this quilt creates the illusion of a much more complicated project in very few seams. Play with color combinations, tile arrangement and size to create a really wide variety of projects from one simple block design.

SUPPLIES

Total of 3–5 yds (2.7 m–4.6m) of fabric for the quilt top, divided up among four to twenty fabrics (see some of the variations on page 54 to get a better idea of how different numbers of fabrics change up the finished look of the quilt).

Matching thread

Quilt batting in the size needed to make the desired finished quilt (see page 57 for a discussion on types of batting)

½ yd (0.46 m) of coordinating fabric for your binding, cut into 2½" (6.4cm)-wide continuous bias tape

3–5 yds (2.7 m–4.6 m) of fabric for the quilt back (this can be larger cuts of fabric or leftovers from the front stitched together; see the samples on page 54 for ideas).

Cut Fabric for the Quilt Blocks

Many traditional quilts are divided into sections called "blocks." In the simplest sense, these are smaller chunks of the quilt that are duplicated over and over, then stitched together to form the final quilt. A quilt block, then, is the design that will be replicated to form the finished quilt. As you work through the Paving Stones Quilt, you'll be making a stack of blocks that each have four pieces of various sizes; you'll make more blocks for a larger quilt and fewer blocks for a smaller quilt. The fabric used for each section of each block might not be the same—for example, you might use a green fabric for the rectangle portion in one block and a black for the rectangle in another. Or you might choose to make every block completely identical. The elegance of using a block design with a quilt is that it allows you both a structure for your patchwork and total freedom within that structure to make something different each and every time.

This quilt comes in four sizes. The primary difference between each size is simply the number of blocks constructed for the final quilt. Each block is constructed using the same series of techniques, then rotated within the quilt to create variation.

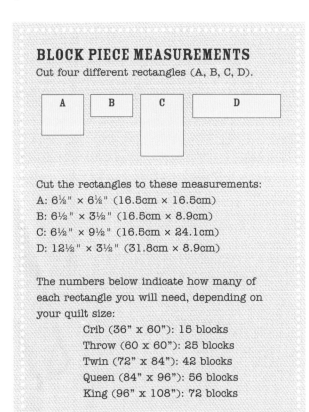

BLOCK PIECE MEASUREMENTS

Cut four different rectangles (A, B, C, D).

Cut the rectangles to these measurements:
A: 6½" × 6½" (16.5cm × 16.5cm)
B: 6½" × 3½" (16.5cm × 8.9cm)
C: 6½" × 9½" (16.5cm × 24.1cm)
D: 12½" × 3½" (31.8cm × 8.9cm)

The numbers below indicate how many of each rectangle you will need, depending on your quilt size:

Crib (36" x 60"): 15 blocks
Throw (60 x 60"): 25 blocks
Twin (72" x 84"): 42 blocks
Queen (84" x 96"): 56 blocks
King (96" x 108"): 72 blocks

CUT BLOCK PIECES

Begin by cutting each of the pieces using the chart as your guide for measurements and number of pieces.

Some folks really like to use sticky notes or custom pins to mark each piece—I think it's a great way to keep track, since a lot of these cuts begin to look very much alike once you get to working with them. Simply write the piece number and letter on a scrap of paper or sticky note and pin through the whole stack. As you remove pieces from the stack, place the note back on top of the remaining pieces in the stack.

TRY THIS, TOO: COLOR VARIATIONS

Like many quilts made from blocks, a simple change in the number of different fabrics used and how many colors are included in this quilt can have a huge impact on the overall appearance of the quilt. Just for starters, check out these three quilts, all the same pattern, but using different fabric combinations.

Yellow and gray quilt: This version uses a very tight color palette, consisting only of citron, gray and a creamy white. There is a wide range of print here—I think a total of over twenty different unique fabrics are represented—but because the palette is so streamlined, the overall impact of the quilt is still cohesive.

Red and black quilt: This version uses a wide range of coordinating fabrics from the same fabric collection, which is to say, from the same grouping of fabrics that were designed to work together. In a collection of fabrics like this, the same print can appear in multiple colors, so while there aren't that many print designs here, there are more colors, resulting in a "busier" overall look to the finished quilt. Note that by rotating the blocks as they're assembled, some of the individual pieces line up with other pieces using the same fabric, making interesting and unexpected shapes.

Green and turquoise quilt: This version uses only four colors, all solid fabrics, and deliberately allows the same color to touch itself when it blocks connect with one another. By using a narrow palette combined with frequent repeat of individual fabrics, you get a quilt that doesn't look anything like the other two, even though it's made using the same design. Consider, as you choose your fabrics, how often you want a fabric to share a seam with itself in another block—you'll be surprised at the variety you can get from this one simple block.

Assemble the Blocks

You'll repeat the steps below for the number of quilt blocks you need to complete your chosen quilt size.

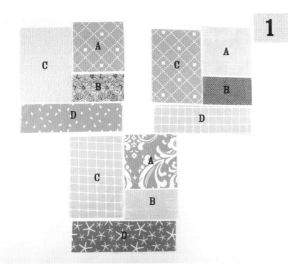

1

1. ARRANGE PIECES

Lay out the pieces A, B, C and D for each quilt block.

2. STITCH PIECES TOGETHER

Stitch the pieces A, B, C and D together using short seams. It's important to stitch the pieces in order: First, stitch A to B, then press the seam allowances to the side, toward the darker fabric. Next, stitch the A/B piece to C, again pressing the seam allowances to the side. (All seam allowances should be ¼" [6.4mm].) Finally, stitch the A/B/C piece to D; press again.

2A

2B

STITCH TIP

See the section on page 51 for a discussion of the pros and cons of pressing quilting seams open.

Assemble the Quilt Top

A quilt top is simply the upper layer of your quilt. In this case, and in most cases, this is the patchwork portion, and is made of the individual blocks you've been sewing. To assemble the quilt top, lay out all your blocks. By rotating and changing the orientation of blocks that border one another, you'll easily be able to create the illusion of a much more complicated quilt without having to do any extra work! Rotate to your little heart's content here, and get everything right where you like it best. Check out the variations below for some ideas.

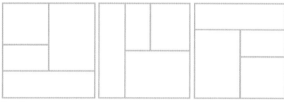

Fig. 1

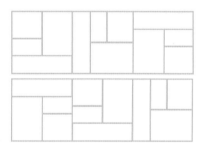

Fig. 2

1. STITCH BLOCK IN EACH ROW

With your rows set in place, begin stitching the blocks together, working across the quilt: stitch one block to the block on its right, then repeat until you've worked your way across the entire row (see Fig. 1). Repeat until all blocks have been stitched into rows. Press all seam allowances to one side. (All seam allowances should be ¼" [6.4mm].)

2. STITCH ROWS TOGETHER

Now stitch each row to the one below it (see Fig. 2), this time pressing seam allowances open.

3. SQUARE UP TOP

Square up your quilt top to ensure the best results. Do this by tugging gently on opposing corners and releasing. The fabric will pop back into place along its woven lines (assuming the pieces were cut on-grain-ish) and you'll avoid a distortion that could make you nuts later on.

THE APPEAL OF LARGE-SCALE PATCHWORK

Don't be intimidated by the idea of making a whole quilt right off the bat! It can be hugely satisfying to make something bigger, something that makes folks say, "WOW!", something that is totally recognizable to even the most uninitiated non-stitcher. If you thought quilting would work best by beginning with an itty-bitty project and working your way up... well, you weren't wrong necessarily, but I say if you're going to go to all the trouble and work through all those steps, might as well really go for the gold, yes? Seeing something that measures five feet square looks impressive, but because quilting allows you to break the work up into stages—piecing the patchwork in sections, then making the quilt sandwich, then sewing the quilting stitches, then binding the quilt—you can pick up and put down your project as you go, until you get an amazing final product. I know you'll love it. Have faith!

Make the "Quilt Sandwich"

This is the part where we take the quilt backing fabric, batting and the quilt top you just made and layer them all together—like a sandwich—and stabilize them before sewing the quilting stitches.

Choosing Batting

Batting is a fluffy layer that gives the quilt its loft and insulation. It also provides a medium for the quilting stitches to create a pattern. Use any type of batting you choose, but consider the options in the sidebar to the right.

Prepare your batting by selecting a piece that is larger on all sides than your quilt top—the patchwork you've just completed.

QUICK GUIDE TO BATTING

Different textiles can be used to make batting, and each one has various benefits and characteristics. Check out this quickie guide to help you make an informed decision as you choose your batting!

Cotton batting: this is the most commonly used in modern quilts; it has a nice loft, is reasonably warm, hand-quilts easily and generally is dreamy to work with; it also "puckers" nicely in the dryer in a way that is very desirable these days.

Wool batting: is very breathable and works well in both winter and summer quilts; hand quilts like a dream; can be expensive.

Silk batting: is exceptionally warm and lightweight, but because the fibers are so dense, can be tricky (if not impossible) to hand-quilt; expensive, but a lovely choice for a deep-winter quilt.

Bamboo batting: a "green" choice, bamboo behaves much like cotton, to the point that I'm not convinced the higher price tag for bamboo is worth it; there are organic cotton options on the market that seem just as good.

Polyester batting: much higher loft than you will see with cotton or bamboo battings, to the point that poly is reminiscent of 1980s comforters; a traditional look that doesn't pucker when laundered; not very popular among the more modern quilters, who tend to prefer natural fibers.

Prepare Backing

The quilt back or quilt backing is the fabric on the bottom layer of your quilt, the back side of your work. Prepare your quilt backing by cutting a piece of fabric that is larger on all sides than the batting and quilt top. You might find that you can't do that with a single piece of fabric, and need to piece the quilt back. This can be all the same fabric, sewn together to make a bigger piece that looks continuous (as I did on the backing shown on page 62), or this can be various fabrics but in bigger chunks, to make a pieced back.

1. SECURE BACKING ON WORK SURFACE

Lay the quilt backing right-side down on a large, clean, flat surface—I use my hardwood floors, but a kitchen floor (or even a bathroom floor) will do in a pinch. Use large painter's or masking tape to secure the edges of the backing, keeping it nice and taut on the floor—almost (but not quite) stretching the fabric.

2. PLACE BATTING AND QUILT TOP

Place the batting on top and smooth it out nice and clean with your hands, leaving no bumps or bubbles. Do the same with the quilt top, right side up, making sure it's plenty smooth. Your backing and batting should extend beyond the edges of your quilt top by at least one inch on all four sides.

3. PIN BASTE

Pin baste by placing large safety pins through all the layers, then back up through the quilt top, and closing them. Pins should be placed about 3" (7.6cm) or so apart across the body of the quilt top, nice and clean. (By the way, I prefer to pin baste rather than spray baste for larger projects. I feel it gives me more control and less mess for less money—obviously, if you've never met a can of spray basting that you don't like, you go on ahead and do it.)

Quilting

For this first quilting project, we'll use your walking foot to put in some clean, straight lines across the body of the quilt. This will give you experience manipulating the quilt as you sew, and keeping your quilting lines straight—don't chomp at the bit just yet, because we've got some fancier quilting going on in later projects. Now attach your walking foot to your sewing machine. (If you don't have a walking foot, no worries—you can still do the quilting, but you may find that you get small "drag lines" across the back of the quilt that result from unequal feed; this is what the walking foot is best at preventing, and what makes it such a nifty tool.) For basic walking foot etiquette, see the sidebar below.

MARK LINES; QUILT

Begin by marking a diagonal line across the center of the quilt at a 45-degree angle. Draw it on using chalk or vanishing ink pen. Beginning at one side of the quilt, stitch with the toes of your walking foot on either side of the line you've marked, and the line centered beneath the needle. Stitch your first row of quilting stitches through all three layers. For the remaining quilting lines, use the guide bar on your walking foot, set to about 3" (7.6cm)—for most types of quilt batting, this is the farthest apart your quilting lines can be set and still guarantee that you won't get any bunching or buckling. Continue to quilt across the quilt at regular intervals until you finish the whole thing. You'll need to figure out the best way for you to manage the bulk of the quilt as you work—you can use clips to roll the body of the quilt up to get the excess out of the way, and at some point most of us throw the bulk of it across one shoulder and "wear" the quilt as we work. You can see why so little quilting gets done in July.

Trim the batting and backing to the edge of the quilt top.

USING THE WALKING FOOT

The walking foot (also called the dual-feed foot, which is shown in the photo above) is another specialty presser foot that's primarily associated with quilting (although I also use mine quite a bit for garment sewing). Don't get distressed—quilting isn't all about special equipment, and you can totally do the quilting on this project if you don't have a walking foot. The benefit of the walking foot is the way it prevents "drag" lines: lines on the back of the quilt that reveal the way the fabric on top of the quilt was "pushed" along as you were sewing. Because the walking foot has feed dogs above the fabric that work in concert with the ones in your machine, below the fabric, you get equal feed that prevents drag lines. The other nice bit about the walking foot is that it allows you to attach a guide bar to make all your straight-line quilting stitches equidistant and parallel to one another. When attaching your walking foot, be sure that the "fork" lever on the right attaches to the screw that holds in your needle on the needle bar of your machine—this triggers the upper feed dog mechanism and ensures you're actually getting the dual-feed capability.

Binding

Cut a length of bias tape to bind the edges of your quilt. You can, of course, use cross-cut strips of fabric, if you prefer—the jury is still out on which is "better," and really it comes down to a matter of preference. Since I think making continuous bias tape (see page 10 as needed for explanation) is akin to a hot night at a dance club, I lean toward bias tape. As a mother of four children, I have no issue with using cross-cut strips when demands of time and family warrant. You do what you like.

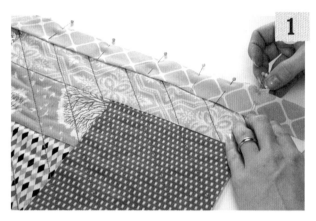

1. CUT BIAS TAPE, PRESS AND PIN ON QUILT

For this quilt, and for most of my quilts, I cut my binding to 2½" (6.4cm) wide. You'll need a single length of binding that is at least 4" (10.2cm) longer than the total perimeter of your quilt, so add up the length of the four sides and add 4" (10.2cm), then make a strip at least that long. Odds are you'll have to stitch some shorter strips end to end in order to get there.

Once you've done that, press in half, wrong sides together with raw edges even. Place the raw edges even with one edge of the quilt—I like to start in the middle of one edge so I can make a clean finish later. Pin along the edge until you get to the corner.

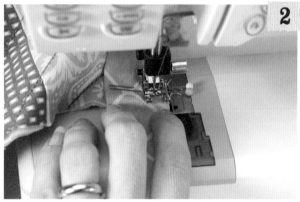

2. STITCH EDGE, STOPPING BEFORE CORNER

Take everything to the machine, and place the raw edge under the presser foot at ¼" (6.4mm) seam allowance. Start about 4" (10.2cm) past the loose end—you'll want to leave that free for now so we can fiddle with it later. Backtack, then sew a ¼" (6.4mm) seam along the edge of the quilt, stopping ¼" (6.4mm) before you reach the corner and leaving that little bit unstitched. Backstitch ¼" (6.4mm) before you get to the corner. As you attach your binding, you can use either your walking foot or your ¼" (6.4mm) presser foot. Some folks feel that the walking foot gives smoother results (when I'm binding with bias tape, I agree with them). Others prefer the accuracy and familiarity of their ¼" (6.4mm) presser foot. In the end, choose the presser foot that will give you the results that make you most satisfied.

3. FOLD THE CORNER

Remove the quilt from the machine and lay the edge flat. Take the binding that's hanging off the end of the quilt, past where you backstitched ¼" (6.4mm) before the corner. Fold it AWAY from the next edge to be sewn, making a triangle from the folded binding.

4. FOLD BINDING TOWARD NEXT EDGE

Now, fold the binding strip back TOWARD the next edge to be sewn, lapping it back over the corner and getting the fold nice and even with the previous edge. You ought to have a teeny triangle flap thingy here, made from the folds you just did—this is totally correct, and will serve to give you a very pretty mitered corner when the binding is complete. Hang in there. . . .

5. STITCH NEXT EDGE

Beginning at the very edge of the quilt, where the folded binding overlaps itself into that triangle, begin sewing another ¼" (6.4mm) seam, taking care to backstitch on the triangle. Sew all the way along this edge of the quilt, attaching the binding as you go, until you get to the next corner. Stop ¼" (6.4mm) before the corner, then repeat the last two steps. When you've gone around the entire quilt and are back where you began, STOP about 4" (10.2cm) before you get to the end of the first section of binding—we'll need to make a clean finish here, and that demands that the ends be left free for now.

6. PLACE ENDS TOGETHER

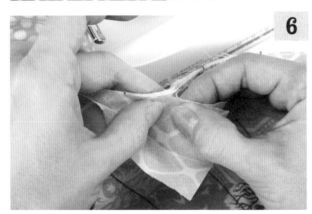

To fuse the two ends of the binding together and make a clean edge, we'll sew a short little seam here. Take the two ends of the binding, both of which should be loose at this point. Open them out so they're no longer folded, then place the ends right sides together. Draw up any slack so the binding will lie flat against the surface of the quilt, then mark the point at which the seam should go to make the binding exactly the right length to finish this edge off neatly.

7. STITCH

Take the binding ends to the machine and sew across the unfolded sections to make a single piece of binding—this might take a couple of tries to remove any extra bulk or length from the binding, but it's worth it. Press the seam allowances open and trim any excess.

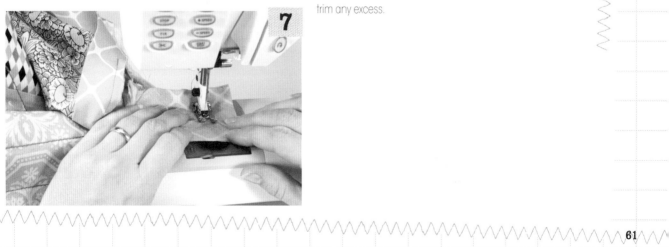

8. COMPLETE STITCHING

Once the binding is the correct length, simply complete sewing it using a ¼" (6.4mm) seam allowance, as you did on the remainder of the quilt. Be sure to backtack at the beginning and end of this seam, overlapping your previous stitches to eliminate any gaps or holes.

WEARING YOUR QUILT

In some cases, quilting and binding will require you to "wear" your quilt, especially if you're making a queen or king size! Feel free to toss chunks of it over your shoulder, but also consider doing these steps on a larger table, where the body of the surface can support the weight of the quilt, or adding a tray table next to your machine to support the quilt. Too much dragging can affect the quality of your quilting stitches or the accuracy of the binding.

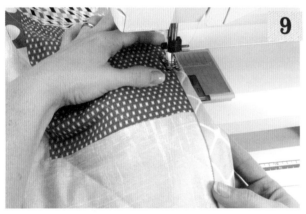

9. STITCH BINDING TO BACK OF QUILT

The final step in completing your quilt (the FINAL STEP!) is to machine-stitch down the binding. First, fold the binding around to the back of the quilt, taking care to extend the folded edge until it's just beyond the line of stitches you just put in. You want to work to have roughly equal widths of binding on the front and back of the quilt—in this case, about an inch (2.5cm). Pin or clip in place (those office binder clips work great here, and there are a number of specialty clips sold exclusively for this purpose), then begin sewing. I like to do mine just to the inside of the binding, about ⅛" (3.2mm) in, using my standard foot. Many folks use their walking foot, to be extra careful they don't mar their binding, which is always a good idea. Go around the entire edge of the quilt, keeping that stitch line as super consistent as you can, and backstitch at the end.

HAND-SEWING THE BINDING

Most traditional quilters hand-sew their binding in place. This can be a longer process than machine stitching it, but in addition to the fact that it's nearly invisible, it's truly gratifying and rewarding work. Plop in front of a movie or among a group of friends, and simply fold or clip the binding to the back of the quilt, covering the machine stitches, then use a slipstitch or whipstitch to anchor the binding in place. These are tiny little stitches, but the results are so lovely! For more detailed instructions, work your way to the **Whole Cloth Quilt** on page 84.

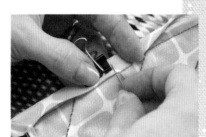

Loving making a bed cover and updating your home's look? A quick-to-make duvet cover will have you rethinking every room in the house! Check out the **Tufted Duvet** (see page 30).

Not all quilts are pieced like this one. If you enjoyed the quilting stitches as much or more than the patchwork, then the **Whole Cloth Quilt** (see page 84) is the perfect next step—another quilt that focuses on the quilting stitches for its look.

NEXT STEPS

LEVEL 2 | SEWING MACHINE COVER

You're probably not taking care of your sewing machine the way you should. Don't get your feelings hurt—most people aren't. Dust and dirt can get stuck in the bits and pieces of your machine and can gum it up and slow it down. The simplest way to keep your machine in its best working order so it will love you back for years to come is to cover it when you're not sewing. This quilted sewing machine cover is custom-made for your little beauty, so you can be just as cool as those dudes with their fancy cars. Adding a touch of patchwork from fabric you really love allows you to have something super pretty that does something super important.

SUPPLIES

1 yd (0.91 m) of solid fabric for the body of the cover

1 yd (0.91 m) of cotton batting, can be fusible

Scraps of cotton prints at least 4½" (11.4cm) square for the patchwork

Thread to match the body fabric

2 yds (1.8 m) of piping filler cord, [6/32]" (4.5 mm) or smaller

Contrasting fabric made into bias tape, 5 yd (4.6 m) total (½ yd [0.46 m] will make enough)

Prep the Patchwork

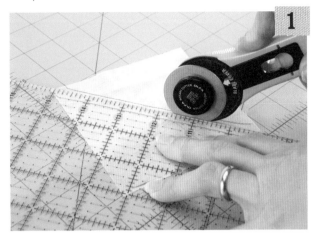

1. MAKE AND THEN DIVIDE HALF-SQUARE TRIANGLES (HST)

Begin by cutting your print fabrics into squares measuring 4¼" × 4¼" (10.8cm × 10.8cm). For the average sewing machine, you'll need nine to twelve squares of this dimension. Repeat with the same number of squares in white fabric (or a color or print to match the body of the cover).

Pair one print square with one solid square and make a half-square triangle (see the sidebar on page 6). Cut the two halves apart on the cut line to divide your HSTs. Press seam allowances to one side. Repeat until all your squares have been paired.

2. MAKE AND THEN DIVIDE QUARTER-SQUARE TRIANGLES (QST)

Mix and match your prints until they're pleasing to the eye, and then pair your HSTs up to make QSTs (see the sidebar on page 7). Cut the two halves apart on the cut line to divide your QSTs. Press seam allowances to one side. Repeat until all your HSTs have been paired into QSTs.

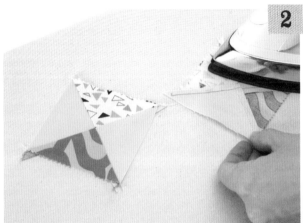

3. ARRANGE QSTS

Stack your QSTs one above the other to make a column, arranging them until you're happy with how the prints relate to one another—not too many pink prints together, not too many of the same fabric right up next to one another, a good balance of light and dark, that kind of thing. I have oriented my pieces so the prints are to the east and west, with the solid to the north and south, because I like the way the little resulting bow ties "float" in the negative space of the solid fabric. Feel free to rotate these for a slightly different look, if you choose!

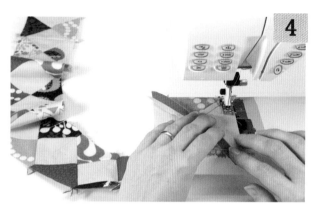

4. STITCH SQUARES

Sew each square to the next one in the column until you have one long strip of patchwork. Press your seam allowances open. Your finished patchwork strip should measure 3½" (8.9cm) wide, with each QST square measuring 3" (7.6cm) high (if not, no biggie—it's a sewing machine cover, after all, and we're about to pop this patchwork strip into another piece of fabric, so you'll have plenty of time to customize the fit).

THE HALF-SQUARE TRIANGLE

Half-square triangles, or HSTs, are a core skill in patchwork and represent you moving quickly from beginner piecing skills right on up to intermediate. Look at you go! To make HSTs, we'll use a little trick that will make your chest puff out with importance, and everyone can use a little of that now and again.

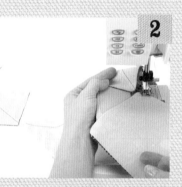

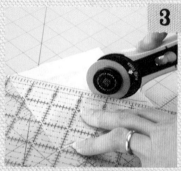

1. Begin with the squares cut to size. Taking one square of your background fabric and another of your print, place them right sides together. Draw a line from corner to corner, diagonally across the wrong side of one square—it doesn't much matter which, but I usually do the solid.

2. With the fabrics clutched together (pressing and steaming them slightly can hold them well), take your squares to the machine. Stitch a seam ¼" (6.4mm) from the line you drew—place the line at the edge of your ¼" (6.4mm) presser foot as a guide. Then, stitch a second seam to the opposite side of the drawn line. HSTs are a great chance to assembly-line your patchwork with some chain stitching. See the sidebar on page 67 for hints on how to make it happen!

3. Back at the cutting mat, cut along the line so you have two squares each composed of a solid triangle and a print triangle. Press your seam allowances.

THE QUARTER-SQUARE TRIANGLE

Quarter-square triangles (or QSTs), the experienced older cousin of the HST, are made from two HSTs sewn together.

 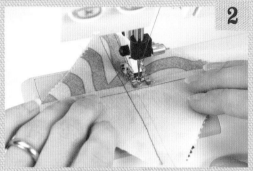

1. Begin with two HSTs (that is, a square piece of fabric made up of two HSTs), and place that piece right sides together with another square of HSTs with their seams directly on top of one another. Be sure to arrange them so that the solid is touching a print on each side of the seam. Draw a diagonal line from corner to corner perpendicular to the seam—it should cross the seam at the center, not be parallel to it.

2. Sew ¼" (6.4mm) seams to either side of this line, as with the HST. Then cut along the line you drew. You'll end up with two squares made up of four triangles, each of which has one small triangle of each of the fabrics in your HSTs.

CHAIN STITCHING

Chain stitching is a handy trick that can speed up your piecing and patchwork by allowing you to avoid cutting threads and lifting your presser foot in between seams. To chain piece, begin by sewing a seam. Then, instead of taking the sewing off the machine, allow it to go past the needle and slip the next piece to be stitched under the toes of the presser foot, taking care to avoid letting the two pieces overlap. Now sew the next seam. You'll find that the "air" between the two pieces is "invisible" to the machine—your needle goes right over it as though there is no gap at all! Now the two pieces are connected by a short piece of thread, just three or four stitches' worth. You can keep adding seams, all connected by a bit of thread, until you're done. Then remove them from the machine and snip the threads—easy! If you're making a whole boatload of HSTs, try stitching all the seams on one side of the center, diagonal line with chain stitches, then turn it all around and stitch all the seams on the other side of the line the same way. Fast and easy!

Assemble the Center Panel

For this cover, we'll need to measure your machine and then use those measurements to determine the overall size of your cover—this is a customized project, after all. So, grab your measuring tape and let's go!

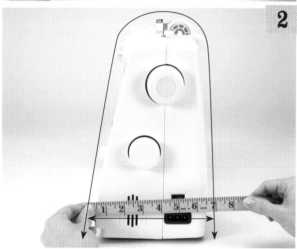

1. MEASURE WIDTH AND HEIGHT

Start by measuring the front of the machine. Measure the width (from side to side, taking into account any little bits that stick out like a cord or spool holder) and the height from base to top (shown here), again taking into account anything that might stick up.

2. MEASURE DEPTH AND LENGTH OVER TOP

Turn to the side of the machine and measure the depth from front to back at its widest point (shown here). Then measure the length over the top of the machine, from the lower front up over the top then back down to the base at the back. Make a note of these measurements.

Now, to each of the measurements above, add 1½" (3.8cm)—a ½" (1.3cm) for seam allowances (¼" [6.4mm] at each side, for a total of ½" [1.3cm]) and 1" (2.5cm) for ease. Ease is that little extra bit of room that will allow you to get your cover on and off your machine. Make a note of these new measurements, and be sure to differentiate them from the ones without seam allowances!

3. CUT FABRIC AND DETERMINE PATCHWORK PLACEMENT

From your solid (or main) fabric, cut out the following pieces using the measurements you've noted (in parentheses): two large pieces for the center panel (width × over the top); four smaller pieces for the side panels (depth × height). Set these aside.

Take one of the center panel pieces you just cut and cut it in half so you can add the patchwork strip to it. With a ruler and marking pen, determine where in the panel you want to place the patchwork—do you want it centered? Off to one side? Randomly placed? Choose now, and with your ruler, mark a line from bottom to top of the solid fabric. Cut along this line to divide the fabric into two pieces (see Fig. 1). Fig. 2 shows where you'll place the patchwork.

Insert patchwork panel here

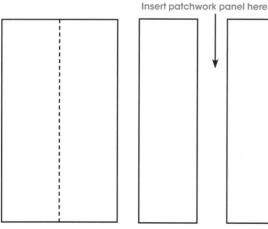

Fig. 1   Fig. 2

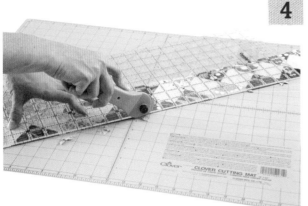

4 **4. TRIM EDGES**

You will find that your patchwork strip has little "ears" from all those seams. Lay it flat on your cutting surface and trim those edges so they're clean and straight.

5. STITCH PANEL

With the center panel fabric pieces right-side up, place the patchwork strip on one panel piece, right sides together and raw edges even. Pin along the raw edge; stitch a ¼" (6.4mm) seam (photo 5a). Repeat with the other panel piece on the opposite long raw edge of the patchwork strip. When you're finished, you should have a panel that looks something like mine does here (photo 5b). Press both long seam allowances open.

6. RESIZE PANEL

Your panel is now substantially larger, yes? So let's trim it back down to make sure that both center panel pieces are the same size. Take the other center panel piece that you cut (in step 3) and lay it on top of the patchwork panel you've just finished. Using the second, smaller piece as a template, adjust the placement of the patchwork strip until it's where you like it best. Then simply trim the excess off the edges of the larger piece so that both center panel pieces are the same size. Magic!

5 A

5 B

Quilting

We'll be treating the center panel of the cover as we would any "real" quilt, so you will basically use the same process you used to quilt the Paving Stones Quilt (see page 52), but on a much smaller scale, of course.

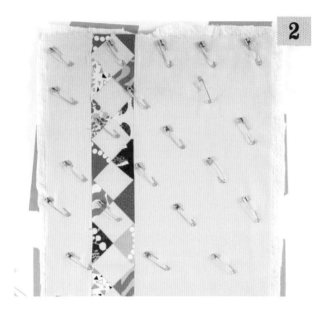

1. CUT BATTING

Begin by cutting your batting. You'll need ONE piece cut the same size as your center panel pieces (width × over-the-top measurements) and TWO pieces the same size as your side panel pieces (height × depth measurements).

2. MAKE QUILT SANDWICH

Make a quilt sandwich using the solid piece of fabric (the "backing"), the batting, and the patchwork (the "quilt top"). Pin baste together. (See page 58 in the Paving Stones Quilt for a refresher on this process.) Repeat this step with the two side panels. Set all three pieces aside as you prepare to quilt.

For the center panel, which we'll quilt first since it's the funnest and most colorful, we'll be combining straight-line quilting with free-motion quilting (FMQ). Both have their advantages and their place, and both are core quilting skills to have in your toolbelt. Let's tackle the straight-line quilting first, since you're familiar with that process from quilting the Paving Stones Quilt, and we'll work our way up to FMQ.

3. MARK QUILTING LINES

Begin by placing the center patchwork panel right-side up on a flat surface. Using a ruler, mark a line across the body of the panel near the center that runs parallel to one of the diagonal seamlines in the QSTs you created. Make sure the line runs all the way from side to side across the center(ish) of the panel—we'll be working outward toward the edges from this line.

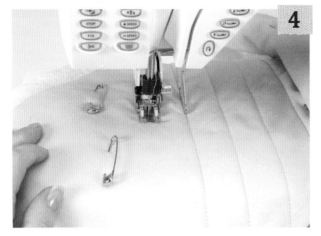

4. START QUILTING ALONG LINES

With the toes of your walking foot on either side of the line you've marked, stitch your first row of quilting stitches. Stitches at the very edge of the quilt sandwich will be hidden in the binding later, so be sure to start as close to the edge as you reasonably can to ensure that you don't have chunks unquilted later.

Then, using the guidebar on your walking foot, continue to stitch rows of quilting stitches parallel to the first line, working your way across the panel sewing each line of quilting in the opposite direction of the previous one. The distance between lines is completely up to you—I set my guidebar to about 1¼" (3.2cm) because I love the narrow look of those parallel lines, but you could set it to a measurement you prefer. "

5. TURN AND CONTINUE QUILTING

After a few rows of this, you'll begin to find that the shape of the center panel is awkward to continue to push under the arm of the sewing machine—that's cool, because we want to leave a corner section without straight-line quilting so we can go back and add a free-motion quilted detail. Stop making straight lines when you're ready (I might suggest going until you've stitched straight lines past all the QSTs on one end of the QST strip, just for continuity).

Remove the panel from the machine, flip it 180 degrees, and begin again at the center line, working your way across the panel with your walking foot and guidebar, until you've reached the opposite end, again leaving a corner unquilted for later.

PIN BASTING VS. SPRAY BASTING

There is an alternative to pin basting, if you don't really like opening and closing all those pins: spray basting. This involves the use of a spray-on glue product to adhere the layers of the quilt sandwich together as you sew. I don't use spray basting, primarily because I don't like the smell, and I have a tendency to overspray that, when combined with a household of small children, leads to a whole lotta sticky. I also like that I can invest once in my pins and they'll last for years and years, rather than needing to purchase another can of spray baste when one runs out. But folks who don't like to or can't (because of arthritis or other issues) use pins prefer to spray baste, which makes it an option you might want to consider.

Once all the straight rows are quilted, we're ready to complete the two sections you set aside to be free-motion quilted. Check out the sidebar/mini-lesson for tips and techniques for FMQ, and then we'll begin.

6. FMQ CENTER PANEL

Using FMQ, work across the unquilted section of the center panel until you've covered all of it. As you start out with your meandering stitch, keep in mind that we want the stitching lines to be no more than an inch apart at any point, and to avoid crossing stitches. Guide the fabric gently beneath the needle—most folks find that the faster you stitch, the easier this is, but I get that to begin with, that can be intimidating. Just work smoothly and carefully, trying not to jerk the fabric from one spot to the next. Your long-term goal is to make the stitches as equal in length as possible while changing direction and covering some square inch-age, but at the outset, just keeping the line of stitching smooth is pretty awesome. If you find yourself trapped in a corner, try to get to an edge—any edge— where you can exit the fabric and being again someplace where you're not painted into a corner. Quilt the entire section, then repeat on the opposite side.

For the side panels, let's mix it up a bit, shall we? Instead of using the meandering stitch, let's throw the pebble stitch around some. Pebble stitches are made of circles upon circles, and cause sections of the quilted fabric to "pop" up above the surface, creating a cool textured effect.

7. QUILT PEBBLE PATTERN

To create pebbles, simply make a circle with your fabric beneath the needle, going around the circumference once or twice, then move on to the next circle, stitching continuously. It helps to make two circles clockwise and two counterclockwise; alternating makes it go faster. Feel free to go back over sections if you need to, or to squeeze circles of varying sizes between one another, until you've got the entire panel covered. Repeat with the second side panel.

Trim the batting and backing on all three pieces (center pane and two sides) down to the side of the tops.

SECRETS TO FREE-MOTION QUILTING

FMQ has been all the rage of late, and a lot of that is because it looks, well, kind of impossible. I mean, stitches that go all over? That loop back on top of themselves in circles and spirals? Doesn't that have to be super HARD? Not really, no! Knowing how to FMQ is done is 90 percent of the battle. After that, just a few handy tips will have you in tip-top shape.

1. Begin by dropping your feed dogs. With these puppies out of the way, you'll be the one controlling how and when the fabric moves under the needle. Your machine likely has a button or switch, usually located near the bobbin case or on the back side of the free arm, or else it has a small plastic cover that goes over the feed dogs, effectively taking them out of commission (they'll still be doing stuff, but they won't be able to touch your fabric through that plastic shield).

2. Next, switch your presser foot to a darning or free-motion foot (you might also be able to use a machine embroidery foot). The key to the presser foot you use is that it must float ABOVE the surface of the fabric when the presser foot is lowered—unlike in regular sewing, you don't want to hold the fabric in place as you sew; instead, you want to keep it from bouncing up and down while still giving you the control to totally direct it as you choose.

3. With the presser foot and feed dogs all sorted out, use a scrap piece of faux quilt to practice: Take a scrap of cotton for a mock quilt top, another for a backing and sandwich a bit of batting between them. Place your teeny pretend quilt under the presser foot, lower and raise the needle so you can bring the bobbin thread to the top of the fabric, thus avoiding snarls, and you're ready to begin. Most folks find that FMQ goes better when they put some speed on their feet but not in their hands—which is to say, mash down the foot pedal but go easy on how quickly you move the quilt under the needle. This part takes practice—just like driving a car, it took you some time to determine how hard to hit the gas and how quickly to turn the wheel, and this is very similar to that. Practice making loops and whirls and squared-off shapes until you feel more confident. With time, you'll begin to want to work on keeping the length of your stitches as consistent as you can, but to start with, try simply to avoid snarls, to keep the movement of your hands nice and smooth and not to have too many stitches that are crazy long and loose. You'll be fine!

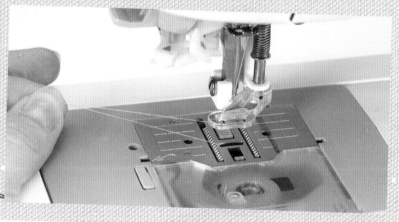

Add the Piping

This sewing machine cover is designed to be reversible, so we'll be piping the seams on one side, and then binding them with bias tape on the other. Begin by creating 2" (5.1cm)-wide continuous bias tape (see page 10, as needed). From that bias tape, make 2 yards (0.91 m) of ³⁄₁₆" (4.8mm) piping (see page 24 for a Crash Course on making piping). Also make 3 yards (2.7 m) of double-fold bias tape (using a bias tape maker—see sidebar below for instructions).

1. PIN PIPING IN PLACE

Trim the seam allowance of the piping to ¼" (6.4mm). Lay one side panel flat on your work surface. Beginning at the bottom edge, pin piping in place with raw edges together and the piping cording toward the center of the side panel. At each corner, snip ¼" (6.4mm) from the edge, up to the stitches but not through them, and "break" the piping to neatly turn the corner.

2. BASTE PIPING IN PLACE

Baste the piping in place by sewing as close to the cording as your machine will allow, using your longest straight stitch. Repeat on the other side panel.

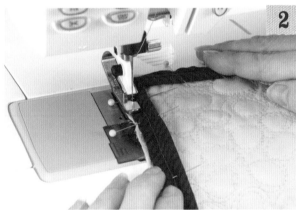

SINGLE-FOLD VS. DOUBLE-FOLD BIAS TAPE

Bias tape is usually pressed and folded to make it easier to apply. When the edges are folded in once, toward the center, this is called "single-fold bias tape," and is generally used to finish off seams where the bias tape won't show on the exterior of the project, like when it's applied to a hemline. When the edges are folded in toward the center, the whole thing is folded in half along the center line. This is called "double-fold bias tape," which is generally used to encase an edge, like when binding a seam.

3. STITCH CENTER PANEL TO SIDE PANELS

Take your center panel and place it patchwork side UP and raw edges together with one piped side panel. (Pin if you like, but I usually don't.) At your sewing machine, stitch a ¼" (6.4mm) seam—right up against that piping cording—all the way around, matching the raw edges and manipulating the center panel as you go, to create a boxed end with the side panel. Repeat with the other side panel. Do NOT clip corners. Remove any visible basting stitches once piping is installed.

Bind the Seams

On the opposite side, instead of hiding the seam allowances from where you installed the piping, we're going to bind them and show them off! Plus, having the bound seam on the inside helps give the additional structure and stability. You'll use your double-fold bias tape for this. (You can use a piping foot here, but a very narrow zipper foot, like I've used here, will do just as good a job.)

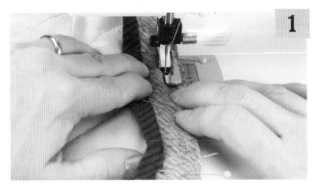

1. STITCH ON BIAS TAPE

Open the double-fold bias tape and lay it right sides together with the center panel at the seam it shares with the side panel. Beginning at the lower edge, pin all along the seam allowance, raw edges even, from lower front to lower back. Stitch in the fold. Repeat on the opposite side.

2. FOLD OVER AND TOPSTITCH

Fold the bias tape over the seam allowance, catching it inside the "clamshell" when the opposite, folded edge of the bias tape lands outside the seam line. Pin in place, then topstitch all along the length of bias tape to bind the seam allowances inside your pretty bias tape. Repeat on the opposite side.

3. HEM

To finish off the lower edge of the cover, repeat the above steps to bind the raw edge. At the beginning, leave 3"–4" (7.6cm–10.2cm) unstitched. When you come back around to where you began, fold the unstitched end under, then lay the opposite end on top. As you wrap the bias tape around to the opposite side, this will prevent any raw edges from peeking out. Topstitch in place and you're done!

NEXT STEPS

Take the idea of reversibles to another level—now that you've made this reversible cover, make the **Reversible Girl's Dress** (see page 132). You can even add trim!

The cutting skills you used to make the patchwork inset for this cover will come in super handy as you prep the pieces for the **Travel Matching Game** (see page 144).

All those clean, straight lines of quilting show up again on the **Reversible Quilted Satchel** (see page 112)—what a great place to keep working on perfecting that skill!

SUPPLIES

Small scraps for the patchwork OR about fifteen charm pack squares (5" × 5" [12.7cm × 12.7cm])

½ yd (0.46 m) cotton batting

½ yd (0.46 m) of cotton fabric, for lining

Matching thread

Walking foot or dual-feed foot for your machine

½ yd (0.46 m) cotton muslin for BACKING (bleached or unbleached)

LEVEL 3 | TEA COZY AND FRIENDS

There are so many, many very cool traditional quilting designs out there that are being given new life with modern fabric and modern colors. Postage stamp quilts are one of those, and represent a spectacular way to use up your smallest little bitty bits of fabric that you love so much you can't bear to throw them away. Mix all those scraps up to make a deliciously random pattern for a tea cozy, or consider narrowing them down to a simpler palette and adding in some solids to give a more cohesive look.

Assemble the Postage Stamp Patchwork

You'll start by cutting your squares. You'll need to cut about eighty-one squares for this project.

1. CUT FABRIC INTO STRIPS

To make the cutting go faster, first cut your scrap fabrics into strips measuring 2½" (6.4cm) wide and as long as you can get them.

2. ROTATE AND CUT INTO SQUARES

Rotate the fabric and cut again in the opposite direction, making 2½" (6.4cm) squares—lots of them. Cool, huh?

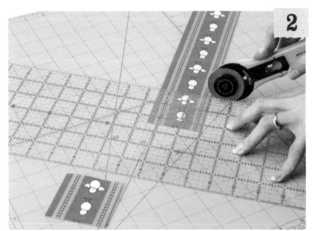

3. ARRANGE SQUARES

Lay out your teeny squares on your work surface and begin arranging and rearranging until you're happy with the overall appearance. Sometimes, it's hard to know what you're really looking for when you go through this step—some folks just push fabric around and cross their fingers. We can do better, so refer to the possible criteria in the sidebar below as you're making your decisions (and then remember that your instincts are way more important than rules).

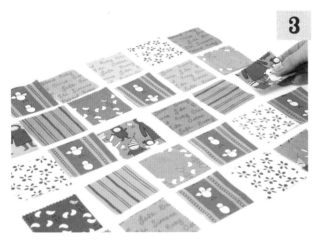

ARRANGING FABRICS FOR PATCHWORK

This is a pretty big topic, but there are some basic ideas that we can cover here. First, think about balancing light colors and dark colors across your patchwork; scatter them about so your eye isn't drawn more to one side or the other. Next, think about balancing color—not too much blue in one section or too much red in another. When working with patterns, think about varying the orientations: A stripe turned horizontally is different from one turned vertically; it's like two for the price of one! These guidelines will help you create a balanced piece of sewing for this project, but feel free to throw these suggestions out the window—many lovely patterns are created when you deliberately break the rules!

Once you're satisfied with the layout of your squares, you'll sew them together. I find it easiest to make blocks and then join the blocks, rather than making super long strips and then having to match all those seams.

4. STITCH PATCHWORK SQUARES

Separate your squares into groups of sixteen: four rows and four columns. Stitch each set of sixteen patchwork squares. Stitch the four tiny squares to form four rows and then stitch the rows together. You should have nine patchwork squares when you're done. Refer back to the test strip we did on page 50—these strips are assembled the same way.

5. STITCH PATCHWORK SQUARES TOGETHER

Now, stitch one patchwork square to another by placing them right sides together and matching each seam—the closer those seams match, the cleaner the look, but really, I love that handmade things are frequently imperfect, and a seam off here and there is certainly not going to make your tea colder. See the sidebar below for tips on locking your seams, which will create perfectly matched seamlines and a very neat result.

6. PRESS SEAM ALLOWANCES

Press your seam allowances open, then repeat until all the patchwork squares have been joined to one another into a giant postage stamp square.

MATCHING & LOCKING SEAMS

Matching seams means that when you place two pieces of patchwork together, the seamlines meet cleanly, with no off-set seams that make wonky lines. To so this, as you press your seam allowances on your first strip of patchwork, press them all to the left. On the strip that will be sewn below that, press them all to the right. Now place those two rows right sides together. See how you get a bit of a ridge on the right side of the patchwork? When you place these two strips right sides together, those ridges bump up against one another, which is called *locking seams*. Place a single pin perpendicularly through each seam, and sew together. Repeat until your block is done!

Cut the Pattern

In some ways, this particular pattern is a bit of a dark horse, in the sense that it isn't totally composed of patchwork—we're making patchwork, then treating that like "fabric" and cutting a pattern from it. While I suppose on one level that can be considered cheating, on another, I think it's a great illustration of the versatility of patchwork, and could be a brilliant jumping-off point for using patched fabric to make clothing or home décor items.

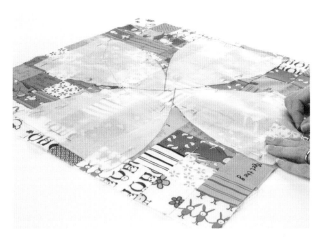

CUT OUT PATTERN

Lay the tea cozy pattern, printed from the enclosed CD, on top of the patchwork panel. Move it around and see if you can't center it on top of your most favorite patches so you'll really, really love the finished product. Ideally, you'll have some patchwork left over for the coaster and the cup cozy, but I would focus here on getting a tea cozy you love and worry about those smaller projects later.

Cut out the pattern, taking care to clip into the points at the heart of the curves, and making crisp ends to each of the petals.

Cut another version of the pattern from your lining fabric.

Double the Batting

The very first quilt I ever made, I took the batting out of the package and was convinced that it wasn't nearly thick enough to make a warm quilt. So I doubled it. And now that quilt is way too hot to sleep under (or sit under, or even sit on sometimes). Batting is super insulating, much more so than you might realize. In this case, though, that's to our advantage, so we're going to use a double layer of batting to make sure your tea stays warm and toasty in its little jacket.

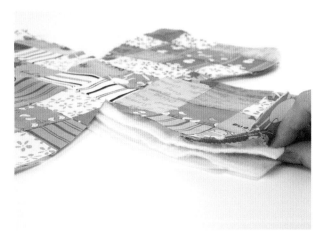

CUT BATTING

Lay out two layers of batting, one on top of the other. Using the same pattern you used to cut the patchwork piece, cut through both layers simultaneously. Repeat with your backing fabric (NOT to be confused with your lining fabric).

Quilting

In the sewing machine cover, we practiced FMQ, making both meandering stitches and pebble stitches. Both of those take advantage of the dropped feed dogs to move the fabric in all directions and get some super cool effects. Here, we'll use that same attribute to do something even cooler: write words in thread as we quilt.

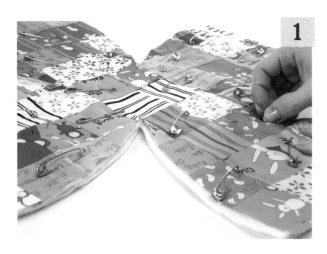

1. MAKE THE QUILT SANDWICH

Baste all the layers of the quilt sandwich together—the patchwork, the two layers of batting and the backing—and bring them to the machine. (See page 57 in the Paving Stones Quilt if you need a refresher on how to make a quilt sandwich.)

Writing Names With FMQ

One of the great things about FMQ is that it allows you to do things with your sewing that would be near-impossible without the freedom of movement it provides. Writing names is one of those things. By using script letters (remember all those handwriting classes in third grade? They are SO about to pay off), you can easily tuck messages, names, secret codes, nearly any text you want into the quilting stitches of a project. They'll be legible, but without being prominent, and it adds such a sweet, subtle touch to your quilting. I've always wondered what it would look like to transcribe an entire poem or letter into the quilting stitches of a project—maybe you can get on that and send me a photo.

2. QUILT THE COZY

Set your machine up for FMQ, either by dropping the feed dogs or covering them with the plate. Beginning at the top of one petal, begin quilting. Using cursive strokes, write individual words, phrases, names or nonsense as you work your way around the body of the quilt, stopping and starting when necessary. Feel free to fill in empty space with meandering stitches, or to connect phrases to one another with random bits of shapes—it all looks great in the end. Try to cover as much area as you can, keeping in mind that the ¼" (6.4mm) at each raw edge will be taken up by seam allowance (so you probably don't want to hide any super important letters there, since they might not be seen later).

Assemble the Cozy

Now that the patchwork and quilting are complete, we can assemble the major seams that make this cozy the perfect hoodie for your teapot. The funny little flower shape is about to come into play, and those curved seams will make a 3D form to cover the height of your teapot.

1. STITCH THE COZY SEAMS

With the quilting complete, lay the cozy right-side up on your work surface. Take one petal and place it right sides together with the petal immediately next to it. Stitch a ¼" (6.4mm) seam along that curved edge. Repeat with all the other petals until you have a dome.

Assemble the backing fabric using the same process.

2. STITCH COZY AND LINING TOGETHER

Place the quilted cozy and the lining right sides together, matching seams all the way around. Stitch a ¼" (6.4mm) seam allowance along the lower edge, leaving an opening to turn.

3. TURN RIGHT-SIDE OUT

Pull the piece right-side out through the opening.

4. PRESS AND TOPSTITCH

Press around the entire hemline. Topstitch the lower edge, catching the opening shut as you do.

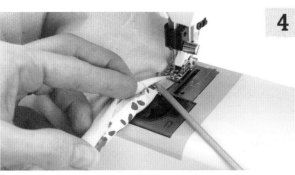

STITCH TIP

If you need a helping hand, use the point of a chopstick or turning tool to tuck the seam allowances back inside the tea cozy to make sure you've caught them as you topstitch.

Make the Coaster and Cup Cozy

The Tea Cozy's friends are simple variations of the cozy. Use the leftover patchwork from the tea cozy if you have it. If not, create new patchwork as you did for the cozy.

Making the Cup Cozy

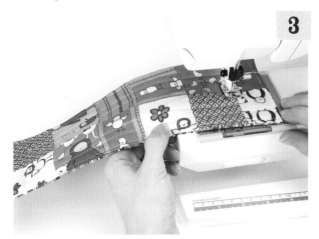

1. MEASURE CUP

Begin by measuring the distance from the inside top of your handle to the inside bottom—we want the finished cozy to fit in that opening. Add ½" (1.3cm) to that measurement. Next, measure the distance around your mug and add 1½" (3.8cm).

2. CUT PATCHWORK TO SIZE

Cut the patchwork to the measurements above: height (distance from top of handle to bottom of handle) by length (circumference of mug plus allowance). Cut batting to the same dimensions, along with backing fabric.

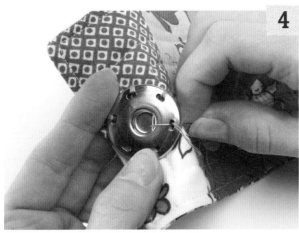

3. QUILT AND BIND

Place the patchwork wrong-side down on the batting. Treating the patchwork and the batting as one piece, place them right sides together with the backing; stitch ¼" (6.4mm) seam around all four sides, leaving a small opening to turn. Flip right-side out, press, then quilt through all three layers. Try starting your quilting stitches along one edge, following the edge of the cup cozy, then pivoting at the corners. Continue in this manner around the entire shape and you'll have concentric rectangle quilting!

4. ATTACH JUMBO SNAP

Hand-sew on a jumbo snap. Place the male half on the side that will be facing out from the mug, and the female snap on the portion that will be facing in. Sew two or three stitches through each opening to secure.

Make the Coaster (a.k.a. Mug Rug)

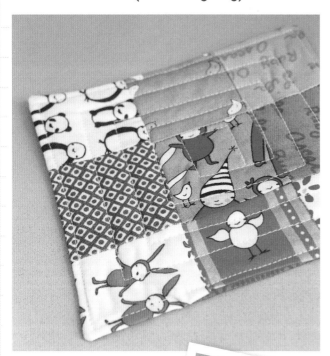

Using a piece of leftover patchwork from the tea cozy, cut a piece that is about 5" (12.7cm) square(ish). Place it wrong-side down on a piece of batting cut to the same dimensions. Treating the patchwork and the batting as one piece, place them right sides together with a solid square of backing fabric; stitch ¼" (6.4mm) seam around all four sides, leaving a small opening to turn. Flip right-side out, press, then quilt through all three layers in whatever whimsical design strikes your fancy.

NEXT STEPS

Making a project that's designed to slip over the top of an existing object sounds like it involves crazy amounts of math, but it's not nearly as intimidating as you might think. Try the **Tufted Duvet** (see page 30) next for more practice!

The beauty of a tea cozy is how it can make you feel warm in anticipation of what's to come. Same thing with the **Lovie Blanket** (see page 138)—the skills you'll need are the same as here, just some simple curves, and the warm glow is like a cup of cocoa.

This project gives you the option of working with fusible fleece. For another project where fusible fleece comes in handy (but can be substituted for quilt batting, just like here), move to the **Fabric Picnic Basket** (see page 106) next and try your hand at a fabric bucket that's adaptable in so many ways.

LEVEL 4 | WHOLE CLOTH QUILT

"Whole cloth" quilts are just what they sound like: quilts that have been made without any patchwork. It's super common for us all to confuse patchwork with quilting, but really, it's the quilting stitches through all the layers of the quilt—quilt top, batting, and backing—that make it a quilt, whether it's been pieced or not. So we're working here with whole cuts of fabric that have no seams. By adding hand-quilted stitches in a regular design across the body of the quilt, we're quilting without having to go through the steps of making patchwork—which gives us the time to really meditate and create something beautiful away from the sewing machine.

SUPPLIES

3 yds (2.7 m) of 60" (152.4cm)-wide batiste or very fine cotton

4 yds (3.7 m) of 45" (114.3cm)-wide white cotton flannel

White thread

Black embroidery floss or perle cotton

Hand-quilting needle

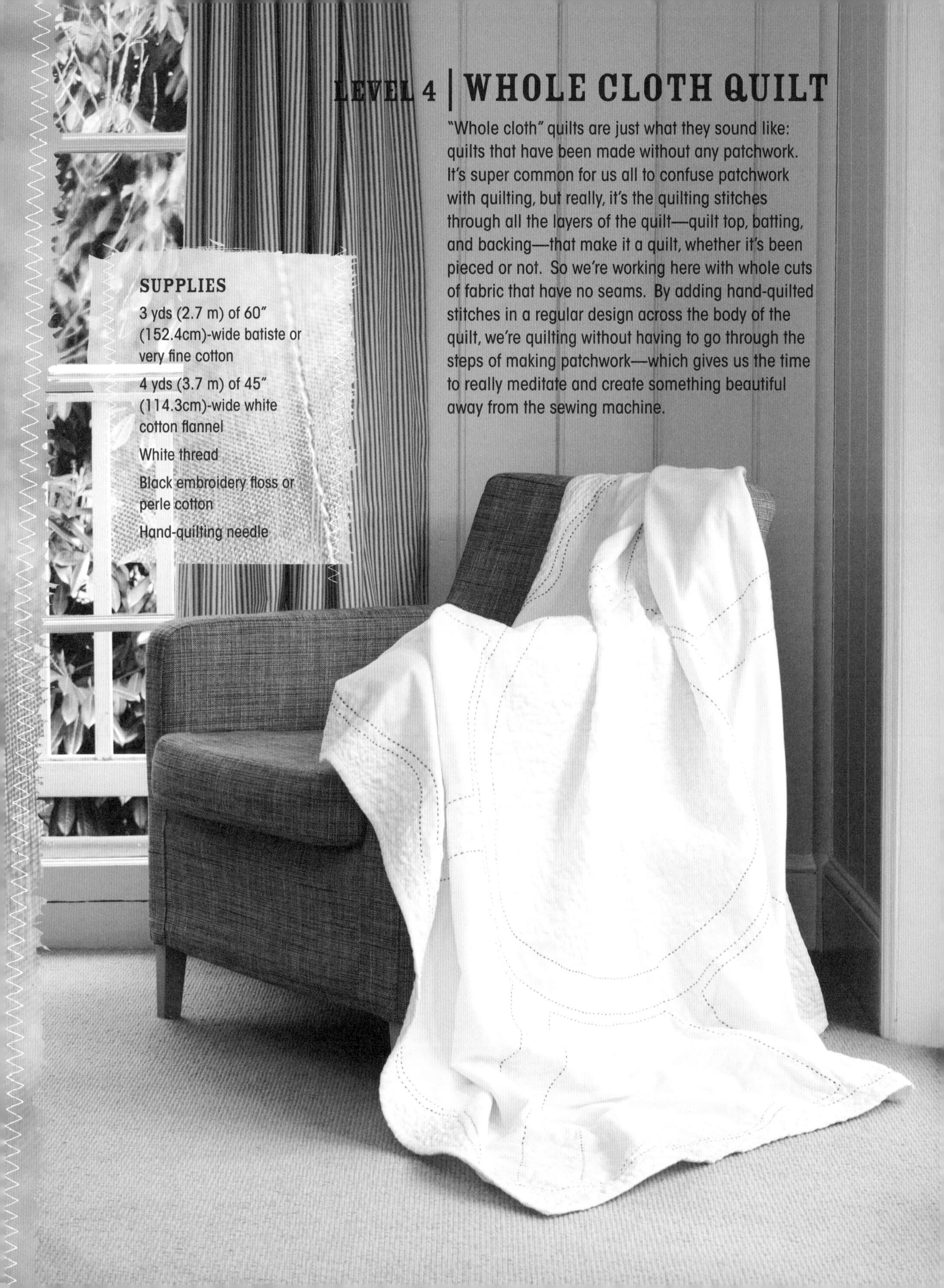

Prepare the Fabric

Most fabrics aren't as wide as you might like for a project like this. We'll be making a quilt that measures 60" × 60" (152.4cm ×152.4cm) finished, and your typical fabrics don't come in these widths. You'll find that the fabrics traditionally associated with whole cloth quilts, such as sateen or batiste, frequently come in widths up to 108" (274.3cm), making larger whole cloth projects easy. For this project, you can choose any fabric on the market that measures at least 61" (154.9cm) wide. Also, keep in mind that most traditional whole cloth quilts would use the same fabric (often from the same bolt) for the quilt front and back.

Before you begin, remove the selvages from your fabric and prewash. When cutting, work with the width of your fabric, whatever that is; it ought to be 61" (154.9cm) square, but there's some wiggle room here. You will need two pieces of fabric cut to these dimensions—one for the quilt top and another for the backing.

Trace the Quilt Design

Traditionally, whole cloth quilts feature a central design surrounded by border motifs and corner accents. The templates on the book CD include a wavy border and spokes that surround a central wheel. You'll fill in with your own vines and stems from there! Mix and match the designs as you please until you're satisfied with the appearance.

TRACE DESIGN ON QUILT TOP

Using a water-soluble marking pen (you might find that the air-soluble ones disappear too quickly for you to get the quilting all done), transfer each design to the quilt top. Many fabrics, like batiste, are sheer enough to see through. Others, like sateen, are thicker—you might try laying the paper on top of the fabric, tracing over each design using a Hera marker, which makes indentations in the fabric along the lines you draw, and then re-tracing those lines with your water-soluble pen.

TRADITIONAL QUILTING DESIGNS

There are at least as many quilting designs out there as there are quilts, really. (Now, don't get "quilt" design confused with "quilting" design—the first refers to the design of the blocks and how they relate to one another; the second refers to the design of the quilting stitches themselves. Traditionally, nature themes have abounded, with vines, florals and waves being very popular, recurrent motifs. You'll also often see geometrics and repeating shapes, as well as symmetrical designs. All of these are represented in this whole cloth quilt, with the aim of demonstrating how even things that might sound super boring and old-fashioned can be very fresh and new when seen with a new eye.

Make the Quilt Sandwich

For this summer-weight quilt, we're going to eschew most of the usual batting choices and go right for something lightweight, durable and unexpected: flannel. Flannel is a great lighter-weight choice that will crinkle nicely in that modern way, but that is easy to get and affordable to sew with. Unfortunately, not many flannels come in the wider widths used in whole cloth quilts, so we'll need to piece our batting. Piecing batting is simple, and in many ways is like doing patchwork: We'll be joining two narrower pieces of fabric to make one wide enough for our quilt. And by the way, we'll be doing this differently from how you might ordinarily seam two fabrics together.

1. STITCH ZIGZAG SEAM AND PRESS

Begin with two pieces of prewashed flannel each measuring 1⅔ yards (1.5 m) long and at least 36" (91.4cm) wide. Press them as crisp as they'll get.

Then lay them out side by side, with edges aligned. Rather than placing right sides together to stitch your seam, you'll be sewing a zigzag seam across the join so that these two pieces can become one with no lump or ridge at the point where they meet. Do this all along the entire length of your pieces using a wide (about 3.5) and long (about 4) zigzag stitch.

Press this seam to set in the stitches before you make the quilt sandwich.

2. MAKE QUILT SANDWICH AND PIN BASTE

Make your quilt sandwich with the quilt top, batting and quilt backing. Remember to lay the backing fabric flat on a large, smooth, firm surface. Secure the backing to the floor, wrong-side up, and then add the batting and quilt top (right-side up).

Pin baste everything in place, placing your safety pins no more than 3" (7.6cm) away from one another. Remember to begin at the center of the quilt and work your way out to the edges, smoothing as you go.

PREWASHING FLANNEL

Since flannel generally shrinks twice (once on the first wash and again on the second), you really do want to wash and tumble-dry it at least one time before using it (some folks go ahead and wash it two times, just to be sure). Without the washing, the batting shrinks and the outer fabric doesn't, making the quilt crinkly. I happen to like that crinkly look, so I just go with washing once.

Hand-Quilting

Hand-quilting involves using a needle and perle cotton or embroidery floss to create the quilting stitches by hand. This makes a wonderful look that can be treasured for years to come, and while time-consuming, is fantastically meditative and gorgeous to look at. The steps are simple, and just a few tricks will help make your work look as though you've been quilting by hand for years.

1. PREP FOR QUILTING

Place all three basted layers in a quilting hoop and secure it (I like a tension hoop, but use a spring-loaded one if you prefer). Thread a hand-quilting needle with perle cotton in any color you choose—if you've selected a white or off-white fabric for the body of your quilt, a contrasting cotton thread can be deliciously unexpected. Thread a single thickness, pulling the loose end through the eye of the needle. Tie a small knot in the opposite end.

2. INSERT NEEDLE AND HIDE KNOT

Beginning at the underside of the quilt, insert the needle at your beginning point—I suggest a straight line along one edge of the design you're quilting. Push the needle all the way through to the quilt top. When the knot comes to a stop on the underside of the quilt backing, gather your courage and pop it through to the center of the quilt, where the knot will be hidden in the batting. This might take a few tries, but once you get the hang of it, it's excellent getting really clean finishes.

3. COMPLETE QUILTING STITCHES

With the thread above the quilt top, place the tip of your needle in the fabric and push it through all three layers—but don't carry the thread below the quilt just yet. Instead, we'll be picking up multiple stitches at a time in order to be more efficient and maintain some stitch-length regularity. Rock the needle up and down, "bouncing" it off your thimble (held below the work), and accumulate four to six stitches on your needle. Work to keep the stitches approximately the same length. Once you've filled your needle, pull it all the way through above the quilt.

Repeat the above step as you work your way around the quilt. At corners, take care to bring the needle up ON the point to avoid having diagonal crossovers on the reverse of the work. Continue quilting the design, tying off at the end of each length of perle cotton and beginning again, always hiding the knotted end in your batting.

Machine Quilting

For the portions of the quilt inside and around the hand-quilting, we'll add some machine stitching to give it dimension and presence. You are free to use those words when showing it off to others, as they make you totally sound like a PRO.

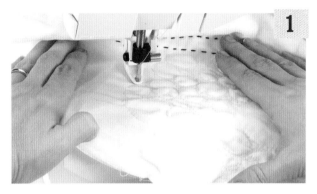

1. QUILT OUTSIDE WITH PEBBLES

For all areas OUTSIDE the wavy line of hand quilting, add FMQ pebbles. Keep in mind that dense quilting like this will slightly shrink the overall size of the quilt. Note that in these images, I'm using a machine embroidery foot rather than a darning foot. For some brands of machine, this is what your free-motion foot will look like.

2. QUILT INSIDE CIRCLE WITH FMQ

For the center of the quilt, inside the circle, add some meandering free-motion stitches. These give visual interest without shrinking or distorting the shapes at the center of the fabric.

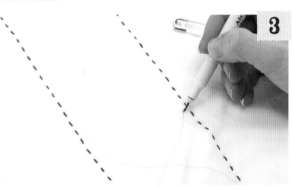

3. SKETCH VINE DESIGN

For the areas inside the "spokes" of the hand quilting, you'll quilt in a vine or rope design—these are traditional elements of whole cloth quilts, and give you a chance to work on some shapes-within-shapes while modern-ing up the technique. There are templates available from a number of designers that you can simply trace into the space you'd like to quilt, or you can sketch in your own design. Here, I'm using overlapping curved lines to mimic a vine. I've sketched with water-soluble ink so I can remove the design if I don't like it, but I can have it last long enough if I need to take a break before quilting.

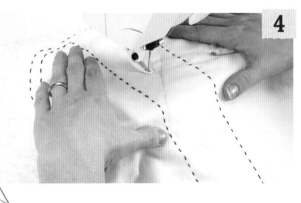

4. STITCH ALONG LINES

Following the lines you've traced or sketched, add the quilting stitches. It works well if you treat these still as free-motion stitches, and use your free-motion foot, as this will give you total flexibility to work within the space you have. Many sewing machines come with an extension table that will give you additional flat workspace around the needle—these are a great investment if you're expecting to make a lot of quilts.

Bind the Quilt

After all the hand-quilting you've already done, it really would be shame to machine quilt the binding on this puppy. Now is the perfect time to hand sew a binding on to create a real heirloom feel and make the stitches on the binding invisible. This also allows your quilting to be the focus of attention on the finished project.

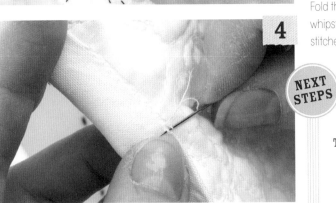

1. TRIM EDGES

Trim the edges of your quilt flush with the quilt top. Make sure that any stray bits of batting and backing are cut away so you have a nice, straight, square edge.

2. MAKE BINDING STRIPS

Make the binding for the quilt by cutting 2½" (6.4cm) wide strips of fabric (either crosswise, from selvage to selvage, or as continuous bias tape) to make one binding strip that is at least 4" (10.2cm) longer than the total circumference of the final quilt. Fold the binding strip in half, wrong sides together, and press.

3. BIND QUILT EDGES

Using the same steps and technique as with the Paving Stones Quilt (see page 52), bind the edges of this project: begin by sewing the binding strip with raw edges even along one side of the quilt, stopping ¼" (6.4mm) from the opposite side; fold the binding strip to miter the corner; continue around the edge of the quilt until you get back to where you began; then stitch a seam in the binding and finish!

4. FINISH WITH HAND-STITCHING

Fold the binding around to the back and use teeny slip- or whipstitches to anchor in place (see the Crash Course on hand stitches on page 122 in the Classy Lady Elbow Bag project).

NEXT STEPS

Simple hand stitches like the quilting stitches you used here can be transferred to the **Sashiko Window Treatment** project (see page 42), where they bring life to a simple curtain.

Like a project with lots of straight lines that doesn't require a ton of cutting? Then move on to the **Ribboned Envelope Pillow** (see page 16) next, and spend your time the way you like!

Heirloom sewing is a class of hand-making all to itself—but really involves loving someone enough to make them something really special. Take your hand sewing-skills over to the **Lovie Blanket** (see page 138) and create an heirloom toy with embroidered details.

LEVEL 5 |
IMPROVISATIONAL
LANDSCAPE WALL QUILT

Improvisational piecing is the term used to describe patchwork sewing that is allowed to evolve with little plan or patterned cutting. This can be organic and based on color or emotion or random chance, or it can be more guided. The basic technique and design for this project came from Sherri Lynn Wood's Mod-Mood Quilt tutorial on her blog, daintytime.net (go check out her blog to see the other amazing possibilities), and is used here with her permission.

My version is intended to ease you into improvisation—which makes a lot of folks a little uncomfortable what with the total lack of pattern pieces and freedom to do pretty much anything.

We're also combining some improvisational piecing with a little trapunto to give it additional dimension and depth. It's pretty cool stuff and an unusual combination, but I'm thinking you'll really like the results.

SUPPLIES

15–20 fabrics in varying shades of green; can be scraps or fat quarters

4–6 fabrics in varying shades of blue, for the sky

½ yd (0.46 m) of cotton quilt batting

½ yd (0.46 m) of cotton muslin

½ yd (0.46 m) of cotton fabric for the backing

Matching thread

Walking foot

Polyfill (just a handful)

Trapunto stuffing tool (or a bamboo skewer)

Map Out the Basic Design

What's that, you say? I promised you improv and now we're mapping? Well, yes to both. I like to know a little about where I'm going before I get too far down the road, but nothing says I have to have an itinerary once I get there. We'll be planning a bit as we make color selections and prep our fabric, and then we'll allow our subconscious to take over.

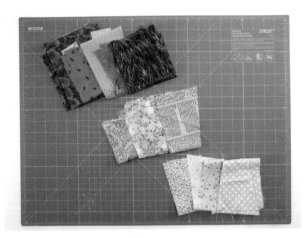

SELECT FABRICS AND ARRANGE

Begin by selecting your fabrics, keeping in mind the colors that you need to create the quilt "picture." (And see the sidebar below for more help.) Much of the layout of this particular design is to emulate a distant hillside or mountain range, so thinking of the colors you'd hope to see in such a setting gives you a great start. Consider that you'd like to have a portion of the image in the foreground, another in the mid-ground and some in the background, and that each of those will have a different depth of color.

Roughly lay out where you'd like to have the completed composition head. For a landscape of this type, the larger an element is, the closer it appears to be to the viewer. You'll want the colors and fabrics you intend to use in the foreground to be larger than those you want to have disappear into the background. We'll look at this in more detail as you cut and begin to stitch.

STITCH TIP

It can be useful to locate a reference image or inspiration photo for a project like this—a quick Google search is a lovely place to start. Or perhaps you have a favorite vacation photo to serve as inspiration.

SUPER BASICS OF COLOR THEORY

Generally speaking, colors fall into two categories: warmth and brightness. Bright colors are those that have more white in them and are arranged on a value scale. Brighter colors appear to be closer to the viewer. Warmth is a measure of how much red and yellow are in a particular color, as opposed to green or blue. Warmer colors are also usually those that pop from a composition and so also feel "closer" to the viewer. When creating a landscape, using this information about color allows you to choose fabrics that will create a more three-dimensional appearance with two-dimensional cuts of fabric. For your foreground, choose fabrics that are bright and warm. For your mid-ground, choose those that are bright but cool, to give a sense of distance. For your background—those objects farthest from the viewer—choose fabrics that are cool and dark, to allow them to recede from the other fabrics and give your composition depth.

Improvisational Piecing

Creating improvisational patchwork is largely built around the idea that with various curves and edges, we can allow fabric to evolve into a shape that we might have struggled to plan consciously. Without getting too touchy-feely, you're letting the fabric have the upper hand, just for a bit, so to speak.

1. CUT WEDGES OF FABRIC

Begin by cutting wedges of each of the fabrics for the hills (foreground and midground), with no plan or template. Vary the length, width and angle of the sides on each piece.

2. STITCH ROWS OF FABRIC

Take the selection of colors of fabric meant for your foreground. Sew one to the other along one raw edge, regardless of whether those edges are the same length. Continue to connect pieces, allowing the patched section to grow into whatever shape shows up.

Repeat with your mid-ground fabrics, then again with your background fabrics. When you finish, you ought to have a series of curves, each patchworked out of multiple fabrics. As you complete each seam, press the seam allowances to the side and very flat.

Lay the patchwork out on a flat surface so you can step back a bit and take a look at the design. Arrange and rearrange the curved sections until you're feeling the magic of the colors and the depth and the variation. Imagine light and shadows, movement and stillness. You can get really deep here, if you want. Or, you know, you can just make it pretty. See how the spirit moves you.

Building the landscape is a matter of creating layers with the curved pieces, then placing them relative to one another so that they create the illusion of distance. It's really a lot simpler than I'm making it sound, so stick with me.

3. LAYER ROWS WITH CURVES

Take the foreground curved piece and lay it on top of the mid-ground curved piece. You want to arrange them so there are no gaps or spaces. It's okay if one is slightly longer than the other—we'll trim it all up when we get there. For now, just place them in relation to one another so you like how the curves and colors relate.

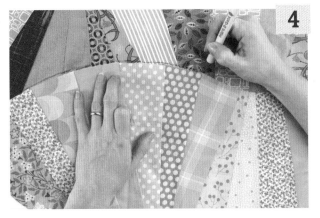

4. TRACE LINE AND CUT

Trace the upper edge of the curved piece onto the background using disappearing ink. Trim out the background along the traced line.

When sewing curved seams, you'll be connecting one concave curve to one convex one. This can seem awkward and tricky, but really gets simple once you've worked with it a bit. If you begin by anticipating that you'll have some excess volume and bulk as you force the two shapes together, you'll have better success in working with the fabric.

5. PIN EDGES

Pin, pin, pin the two edges together, keeping the fabric at the raw edge nice and flat and allowing the volume to fall away to the interior. You'll find that you get lumps and bumps, but so long as those are in the body of the fabric and not in the seam, you'll be okay.

6. STITCH

Stitch the curved seam using a ¼" (6.4mm) seam allowance. This is slightly trickier than a straight seam, but not much. Simply take care that as you sew, you continually move your hand beneath the fabric to get all the bulk out of the way, ensuring that you're only sewing through a single layer at a time. That way, you won't get any puckers or bumps. Press the seam allowances in one direction or the other, but not open—they won't lie flat if you attempt to press them open. Repeat all these steps to attach these two curved pieces to the next curved piece.

Now you'll choose a color for the background (sky) of the quilt—blue would be an obvious traditional shade, but consider sunset colors, or even unexpected colors for a more impressionistic vision of a landscape. What about red? There are mountains on Mars, after all.

7. ASSEMBLE SKY PIECES

Using large pieces of the sky fabric, repeat the process of breaking them into wedges, but this time make those wedges substantially larger than the ones we initially made for the rolling hills and mountain ranges. You'll want four to six large-ish pieces.

Lay your patchwork of curved pieces on top of the sky you've just created. Assemble using the techniques in steps 3–6.

8. TRIM EDGES

Now it's time to get all the excess fabric out of the way and trim the edges. Lay your piece out on your work surface, nice and flat. You have pressed each seam, but if you're still seeing a bit of puckering here and there, hit that bad boy with some steam and see if you can't get it to behave. Then, look at the edges and determine just how large you can make this—I like to maximize my dimensions, if I can. Using a ruler and rotary cutter, trim down the left and right side, as straight as you can. Repeat with the top and bottom, squaring off the whole piece and keeping the corners nice and crisp. Discard the extra bits.

ADDING APPLIQUÉ

For this project, I was going for a more abstract look. But, if you would like to make your landscape a bit more literal, add some appliqué!

To do so, begin by free-form cutting your elements (like trees). Using basic machine appliqué techniques, attach the trunk first and then the branches of the tree to the patchwork.

Quilting

For the quilt, you'll need some cotton quilt batting and backing fabric. This backing will be hidden and you'll use a "real" backing later after we do the trapunto, so this one can be scrap fabric or muslin.

1. LAYER QUILT, BATTING AND BACKING

Cut a piece of batting and a piece of muslin (backing) fabric that measure 1" (2.5cm) larger than the quilt top on all sides. Layer your quilt top, batting and backing together to make the quilt sandwich. Pin baste in place. (Refer to the Paving Stones Quilt on page 52 for a refresher on how to do this.)

2. ADD QUILTING STITCHES

Using a walking foot, quilt through all the layers, stitching parallel to the curved lines at the upper edge of each patchworked piece. This emphasizes the curves and makes those hills really POP. Trim the batting and backing to the same size as the landscape top.

TRY THIS, TOO

If you're familiar with hand quilting, you could certainly hand quilt this baby. Hand quilting would give more texture through the larger thread, and the chance to really add some depth and shading to the landscape without having to learn super-advanced machine quilting techniques.

To hand-quilt, use a #8 pearl cotton and a standard embroidery needle. Begin by marking out the quilting lines with chalk or water-soluble marker (disappearing ink likely won't last long enough). Following the shape of the curves, trace out quilting lines directly onto the quilt top. You could draw them close together and then make them gradually farther apart to give the illusion of increasing distance across the face of the landscape (refer to the previous project, Whole Cloth Quilt on page 84, for detailed instructions on hand-quilting).

Trapunto

Trapunto is a traditional quilting technique that adds dimension and shape to a quilt by introducing additional batting or stuffing through the back of the quilt in strategic places to make it three-dimensional. Generally, the area that will be stuffed is bounded on all sides by quilting stitches (though our project includes stitches just on one side). What a cool way to venture into the world of art quilting, where the goal isn't necessarily to make a quilt that is serviceable, but rather one that expresses an idea, creates a painting out of fabric or simply experiments with shape and form through textiles.

On the backside of this quilt, we're going to slice open the backing behind particular areas of the hillside in order to expose the batting inside. We'll add more batting (polyester fiberfill), to make it three-dimensional.

1. MAKE A SLIT FOR STUFFING

Begin by determining where on the landscape you want to add three-dimensionality—I've done mine behind the apex of each hilltop, to emphasize the illusion that they're rounded and fading into the distance. Using very sharp embroidery scissors (not your seam ripper, as this could get away from you and go right through your quilting stitches), cut a slit directly behind where you want the fullest portion of the stuffing to be, about 1" (2.5cm) across—any bigger, and you'll have a hard time controlling the movement of the stuffing inside the quilt. .

2. ADD STUFFING

Pop in a bit of fiberfill, taking care not to rip the fabric or your quilting stitches. Check the front of the quilt to determine how much stuffing you want to add. But don't over stuff!

Repeat for any and all additional areas of hillside you'd like to stuff. I'd recommend using varying amounts of stuffing, depending on how far away you'd like an element to appear—those with greater shading and three-dimensionality will appear closer than those with less.

Backing and Finishing

Now we'll add the "real" backing. Because we cut into the muslin backing, we don't want to have that as the finished backing on the quilt. Instead, we'll add a new, solid piece of fabric that will serve to both disguise the trapunto and keep the extra stuffing inside.

1

1. STITCH ON BACKING

Cut the backing fabric to the size of the quilt. If you don't have enough fabric, you can piece your backing like I did or just use one big piece. Place the quilted piece right sides together with the backing, and stitch around the outer edge using a ¼" (6.4mm) seam allowance, leaving yourself a small opening to turn. Clip the corners at an angle to remove bulk, then flip right-side out and press.

2. TOPSTITCH

Topstitch around the entire edge, about ¼" (6.4mm) in, catching the opening closed as you do. Consider stitching again slightly farther in to create a "frame" effect to the finished piece.

2

HANGING THE QUILT

I think the best way to hang this quilt and show it off right is the same way you would hang a curtain panel: by installing a short rod on the wall and using drapery clips. Other creative options for handing include: attaching a pretty pants hanger and hanging from a hook; attaching ribbon; installing a rod pocket (as in the Sashiko Window Treatment on page 42).

NEXT STEPS

Balancing color and working with shapes is central to the **Sewing Machine Cover** (see page 64)—take the skills you've used here over there and create a piece of art that's functional and will keep you sewing longer!

Like this project, the **Reversible Girl's Dress** (see page 132) uses curved seams to make the shape of the piece work. Head that way and perfect your curved seams to see how they really elevate your sewing to the next level!

Stuffing is fun! The **Lovie Blanket** (see page 138) lets you use up some of the leftover fluff you might have lying around after this project. Try that one next!

SECTION 3:
BAGS

I'm always surprised at how many people really, really want to sew handbags. And then I remember how many bags and totes and satchels and purses I myself possess, and suddenly I understand. There is an art to bag-making, but since there are really only so many ways to put a bag together, you'll find that the same principles and techniques come up over and over again. These shapes are core basics and will serve you well, from formal situations to the everyday. You might find, as I did, that suddenly all you need are a few basic bag styles, and plenty of embellishments, and you're set for a long while. Two words: matching handbag.

LEVEL 1 | EVERYDAY SHOULDER BAG

I love a small, under-the-shoulder bag that's just the right size to fit my wallet and phone plus a few little bits—but not quite big enough for all the luggage that four children can expect me to tote for them all over creation. Add a little funky fabric for lining, and this bag transforms to something truly special. I strongly suggest making more than one, especially with the extra pop it would get from adding piping.

SUPPLIES

½ yd (0.46 m) of mid-weight fabric for the body of the bag

½ yd (0.46 m) of lighter weight fabric for the lining

1 yd (0.91 m) of piping cording

Bias tape to cover the cording

½ yd (0.46 m) of mid-to-heavy-weight fusible interfacing

½ yd (0.46 m) of light-to-sheerweight fusible interfacing

Matching thread

Cut the Bag and Lining

1. CUT FABRIC PIECES

Cut two of the bag body pieces from your main fabric, and two from the lining. Repeat with bag gusset. Cut one of the bag straps from your main fabric, and two of the tab.

2. INTERFACE OUTER BAG PIECES

Interface the outer bag body pieces with heavy-weight fusible interfacing. The heavier this is, the more firm, so the stiffer you want your bag to be, the more serious you want your interfacing to be. I would caution you NOT to use ultra-heavy duty interfacing, like Peltex or Timtex, as that makes the bag too difficult to work with at the machine. Repeat with the outer gusset.

3. INTERFACE LINING PIECES

Interface the lining of the bag with light-to-sheerweight fusible interfacing. Repeat with the gusset lining, straps and tabs.

ALL INTERFACINGS ARE NOT THE SAME!

Interfacing comes in a lot more varieties than most people think! The biggest difference is fusible vs. sew-in. Fusible interfacing has a heat-activated glue on one side that allows it to bond to the wrong side of your fabric so they can be treated as one while you sew. Sew-in interfacing doesn't have that and will be basted to the wrong side of the fabric. Some fabrics, like silks and such, shouldn't get a fusible, as it doesn't play nicely with their drape, so a sew-in certainly has its place. Most folks tend to rely on fusibles, though, for their everyday sewing.

The weight of the interfacing is the next relevant factor, and this is regardless of whether you're using fusible or sew-in. As a rule of thumb, the interfacing should be slightly lighter than the weight of the fabric; the job of interfacing is to stabilize and give support to the fabric, not to BE the fabric, so your main textile should always have more heft than the interfacing you use with it.

Finally, remember that interfacing comes in colors! Especially on projects that include buttonholes, where bits of the interfacing might peek out, use dark or black interfacing with dark fabrics and light or white interfacing with light fabrics.

Add the Snap

Nothing makes a bag more complete than a good closure. Adding yours now makes the stitches completely invisible and allows you to prep for later. You can choose either a kicky jumbo sew-on snap, or a choose a magnetic snap, which lends such a nice touch of store-boughtness to it.

1. MARK SNAP PLACEMENT; ADD INTERFACING

Place the snap where you want it to be in the finished bag, on the right side of the lining. Allow ½" (1.3cm) from the upper edge of the lining for seam allowance, plus another ½" (1.3cm) or so for "clearance" when opening the bag—that bit of lip that gives you a place to grip as you pop the snap open.

Mark this spot, then fuse a 2" × 2" (5.1cm × 5.1cm) piece of interfacing to the wrong side of the fabric behind the spot where you'll stitch the snap—this will help the fabric avoid tearing when you open the bag.

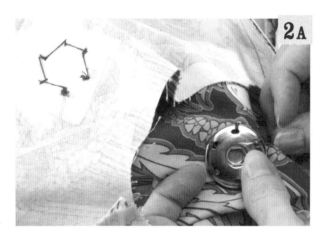

2. OPTION A: SEW-ON SNAP

To sew the snap on, stitch through the holes in the edge of the snap two or three times, bringing the needle back down as close to the original spot as you can. When you're done with one hole, carry the thread over to the next one on the wrong side of the fabric for an invisible finish. Tie a knot when you're done, then repeat on the opposite side of the snap.

2. OPTION B: MAGNETIC SNAP

Push the points of the magnetic snap parts through the lining fabric to the back, then bend them flush. They'll be hidden on the interior of the lining when the bag is complete.

Sew the Strap and Tabs

The straps and tabs here are constructed the same way, and are simple double-turned strips of fabric. Neither of these is lined. You'll need one strap and two tabs.

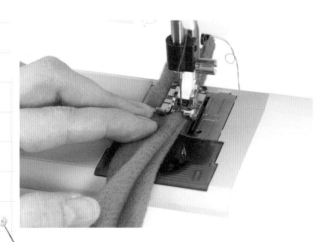

PRESS STRAP AND TOPSTITCH; MAKE TAB

Take the interfaced strap and press each long edge in ½" (1.3cm). Press again in half, bringing the two long, pressed edges together. Topstitch along both long sides. Leave raw ends unstitched, for now.

Form each tab the same way—and remember to make two!

Assemble the Bag

With the snap installed and two body parts for the bag, we want to install a gusset. This is a lower panel, which gives the bag some shape and room for all your stuff—otherwise, the bag would be super skinny and flat, and no one can make that work in real life.

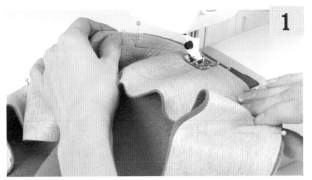

1. STITCH ONE SIDE TO GUSSET

Take the gusset piece of your outer fabric. Pinch-press the gusset to mark the center, and do the same to each side of the bag body. Do this by folding the piece in half and giving it a good, tight squeeze—you'll see that you've left behind a teeny mark, which you can use to match up centers without needing to reach for your chalk! (I love me a good time-saver.) Make a similar pinch press at the center of each of your outer bag sides. Place one bag side right sides together with the gusset, matching up those center pinch pleats. Sew a ½" (1.3cm) seam from the center toward the edge, then sew a second seam from the center toward the other edge. By beginning in the center, you'll make sure that any excess fabric doesn't get bunched up at the middle of the bag and leave an unintended pucker.

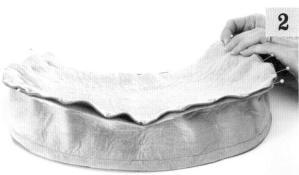

2. STITCH OTHER SIDE TO GUSSET

Pin the other side and stitch. Repeat on the opposite side of the bag, so you have a gusset in the center that is attached to the bag sides.

Repeat again with the lining.

3. CLIP CURVES

On both the outer bag and the lining, clip around the edge up to the stitching but not through it, about every inch (2.5 cm) or so. This will help those curves relax and allow the bag to sit neatly when you're finished sewing.

4. FOLD AND PIN TABS

Before we put the lining and the outer bag together, we'll want to add in the tabs for the bag hardware, so we'll be able to attach the strap when we get to that point. Take one tab and fold it in half. Place a D-ring over one end and leave it pinched in the center of the tab as it is folded.

Pin one tab on each gusset, at the side of the bag. Tabs should have the D-ring hanging down, with raw edges even with the upper raw edge of the gusset.

5. TRAP STRAPS BETWEEN BAG AND LINING

Slide the lining, wrong-side out, over the outer bag so the two are right sides together. The tabs are sandwiched in the middle, with the D-ring caught on the tab. Pin the edge.

6. STITCH EDGE

Stitch a ½" (1.3cm) seam around the entire upper edge of the bag, leaving a small opening to turn right-side out, and catching the tab ends securely in the seam—you can even consider backstitching over the tab ends as you sew past them, especially if you plan to carry super heavy items in your bag, like spare batteries or vintage jewelry. Up to you.

7. TURN RIGHT-SIDE OUT AND PRESS

Reach through the opening in the lining and turn the whole thing right-side out, teasing out the fabric until the whole bag spills out and you're able to stuff the lining back inside. Press.

8. TOPSTITCH

Topstitch around the upper edge to close the opening you used to turn, and to create a finished feel to the bag. Take care as you stitch past your snap!

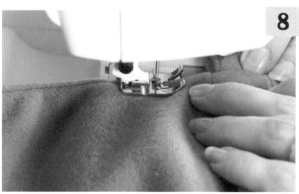

Finish the Strap

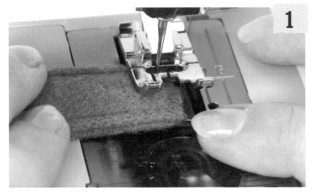

1. SEW STRAP END

Tuck the raw edges back into the opening of the strap and stitch the opening closed. Repeat on other side.

2. STITCH STRAP CLOSED AROUND D-RING

With the bag right-side out, place one end of the strap through the D-ring, then fold it around the D-ring until the folded edges touch the body of the strap. Stitch in place.

Repeat on the opposite tab.

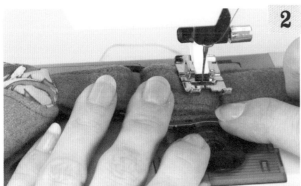

ADDING A POCKET

Want to add a simple pocket to the interior of this bag? Simply stitch your pocket on to the lining before attaching the lining to the gusset—if you wait until after, you won't be able to access the edges of the pocket in order to stitch them down. Order of operations is everything (and you thought you'd never use algebra in real life!).

NEXT STEPS

Ready to sew some more curves, like the ones you mastered on this bag? Check out the **Reversible Girl's Dress** (see page 132) and try some on a smaller scale.

Like working with snaps? If you sewed them on by hand or if you invested in a snaps pliers and want more, move on to the **Travel Matching Game** (see page 144) and you can add a zillion snaps, just for the fun of it!

LEVEL 2 | FABRIC PICNIC (OR ANYTIME!) BASKET

This simple shape can be transformed into nearly limitless containers: organizers for your shelves, baskets for catching the things that rattle around the car (I'm told it fits perfectly between the front seats of a mini-van, just FYI) or a hip picnic basket for taking your bestest lunchy foods out for a trip to the great outdoors. Adding loops and pockets lets you organize so you're ready to invite your closest friends to enjoy the glory of nature while you show off your mad sewing skillz. Whaaat?!? You heard me.

SUPPLIES

1 yd (0.91 m) of mid-to heavy-weight cotton fabric (maybe laminated!)

1 yd (0.91 m) of lighter-weight lining fabric, like a coordinating quilting cotton

18" (45.7cm) square piece of Peltex or other super-heavyweight interfacing

1 yd (0.91 m) of cotton batting

Matching thread

Assemble the Body of the Basket

Start by cutting. You'll notice that the side pieces, both long and short, are slightly shorter than the sides of the bottom piece. That's to allow for putting the four sides on the base without any of them overlapping or getting lumpy.

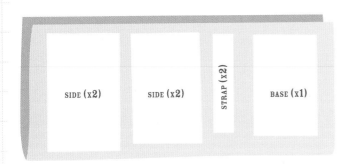

1. CUT FABRIC (OUTER AND LINING) PIECES

Cut the base piece from a heavyweight fabric, like canvas or heavy linen or home dec, measuring 17" × 12" (43.2cm × 30.5cm). Cut two side pieces measuring 16½" × 9" (41.9cm × 22.9cm) and two side pieces measuring 11½" × 9" (29.2cm × 22.9cm). Cut all the same pieces again from the lining fabric.

FOR AN EXTRA-STIFF BASKET

To make your basket a bit sturdier, interface the lining fabric. If you are planning on storing or carrying heavy items in this basket (books, wine bottles, pet rocks) consider adding ultra-heavyweight interfacing (such as Peltex or Timtex) to make it extra stiff. Add this to the outer basket fabric.

2. STITCH SIDE PANELS TO BOTTOM

Take your two long sides, place one right sides together and raw edges even with the base piece, and center the side so that you have approximately ¼" (6.4mm) of "extra" base piece at either side of the centered side panel. Stitch a ¼" (6.4mm) seam allowance through the double thickness. Repeat on the opposite side with the other matching panel. See that teeny overhang at the corners? That's good—we want that.

Now, take the third side piece and repeat, placing the raw edges of the remaining side pieces flush up against the seam you just stitched, and centering the panel on the base piece (as shown). Stitch the side panel with a ¼" (6.4mm) seam allowance. Repeat with the opposite panel.

3. REPEAT WITH LINING FABRIC

Press the seam allowances toward the side panels, keeping the base piece nice and flat. Press again from the right side, opening out those seams so they're really crisp. Repeat all these steps with the lining fabric. At this point, you have two T-shaped pieces that are the same size as one another.

4. CUT OUT BATTING

Lay the T-shaped piece wrong-side down on a piece of batting or fleece (read more about fusible batting in the sidebar on the next page). Cut around the T-shape of your basket and make a duplicate of your batting (all one piece).

USING FUSIBLE BATTING OR FLEECE

Like interfacing, batting comes in a wide variety of formats. One that can be nice for bags and fabric baskets like this one is fusible fleece. This is a polyester product that has heat-activated glue on one side and can be pressed into place to avoid shifting as you sew. I don't love fusible fleece for quilts and the like, but I do love it for a project like this, because it eliminates the need for pins as I'm working, which makes the whole project go more quickly and smoothly. Most fusible fleece can be purchased in small packages, or by the yard at a fabric shop—look for it where you find the interfacing or quilt batting.

For the record, it's about the same level of difficulty whether your batting is fusible or not, so if you don't have access to fusibles, don't sweat it.

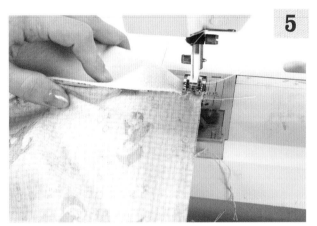

5

5. STITCH SIDE SEAMS

Fuse, if your batting or fleece is fusible. Then fold the T-shape right sides together so that two of your edges come together at the corner. This is how we'll make the sides stand up on your basket. Pinch them where they intersect with the base and begin stitching there, using a backstitch. Sew all the way up the side seam (the image shows only the outer fabric, not the batting, for clarity). Repeat for the other three corners.

6. REPEAT WITH LINING

Now you should have a boxed shape that stands up on its own! Repeat with the lining (except that one probably won't stand up on its own—unless you interfaced it like I did).

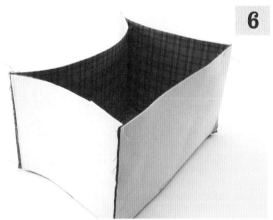

6

Add the Straps

Now for the straps. These are entirely optional, and can match your basket but don't have to.

1. CUT AND SEW STRAPS

Cut two strap pieces that measure about 12" × 2½" (30.5cm × 6.4cm)—give or take. Fold in about ¼" (6.4mm) along each long edge and press. Then fold again in half lengthwise so that the two folded edges lie on top of one another. Press.

Topstitch close to both long edges, catching the strap closed as you do.

2. PIN STRAPS ON LINING

Pin the straps to the basket, right sides together and raw edges even. Spacing is by eyeball—just put them as far apart as you think they'll look pretty. You might want to do a test, though, to make sure you can pull the straps together (if they're long enough) if you're using this as a bag-type basket (and, say, not just for storage).

3. PIN OUTER FABRIC TO LINING, TRAPPING STRAPS

Take the lining, all boxed and seamed at the corners, and place it right sides together with the main fabric, sandwiching the straps between the two, keeping all your raw edges even.

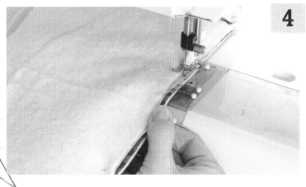

4. SEW UPPER EDGE

Stitch a ¼" (6.4mm) seam all the way around the upper edge, leaving an opening along one side through which you'll turn the basket right-side out. Backtack at the beginning and end of the opening to give it some strength.

Finish

Ready to turn this puppy right-side out and see some magic happen? We're almost there!

1 **1. TURN RIGHT-SIDE OUT**

Go through the opening you left and grasp the outer fabric. Pull it through the opening, bringing the lining along with it, until both fabrics are right-side out.

2. TOPSTITCH SHUT

With the outer fabric and the lining right-side out, tuck the lining back inside the outer basket. Press, press, press all the way around that upper edge to make it nice and smooth, tucking in any seam allowances that are still peeking out from the opening you left for turning your work. Then, topstitch all the way around the upper edge, close to the edge, catching the opening closed as you do. Voila!

2

NEXT STEPS

This fabric basket uses batting to give it shape and structure. Use the same to give softness and warmth to the **Whole Cloth Quilt** (see page 84)—you'll be amazed at how you can take simple supplies and get such different results!

The **Footstool Slipcover** (see page 22) has a lot in common with the Fabric Picnic Basket, just upside down! If you can make this fabric basket, you can slipcover a stool—and suddenly the whole world of home décor is available to you.

Want to take these same skills and take them up a notch? Try the **Lay-Flat Backpack** (see page 150), which is a similar shape and uses the same sewing skills, but adds a zipper and straps to make it really interesting.

LEVEL 3 | REVERSIBLE QUILTED SATCHEL

What's super great about this satchel isn't just the perfect size (because it's pretty close to perfect) or the fact that it's lined-slash-reversible (which makes it really flexible and useful), but that it's so ridiculously simple to assemble. You'll find yourself making a bunch for yourself, then giving them away to those deserving few in your circle who actually are worthy of your sewing time. Want to mix it up? You could pipe it, too!

SUPPLIES

1 yd (0.91 m) of home dec weight or linen blend fabric for the outer bag

1 yd (0.91 m) of home dec weight or quilting weight cotton for the lining/reverse

Matching thread

1 yd (0.91 m) of quilt batting (I like cotton)

¼ yd (0.23 m) of heavy duty fusible interfacing, like Peltex

2½ yd unbleached cotton muslin

1 yd midweight fusible interfacing

Cutting the Bag Pieces

1. CUT FABRIC PIECES

Cut the flap from your main fabric to measure 28" × 17" (71.1cm × 43.2cm). Cut a piece of muslin and a piece of batting to the same dimensions. Repeat for the lining fabric, muslin and batting.

Cut the panel for the sides/bottom of the bag—again, one each of your two fabrics (outer bag and lining), measuring 4" × 19½" (10.2cm × 49½cm). (If your fabric is too short, cut two pieces and add a seam to create the 19½" [49.5cm]. Centering the seam makes for the best results.)

Cut two front panels, one each of your two fabrics (outer and lining), measuring 13" × 17" (33cm × 43.2cm).

Cut two straps, one each of your two fabrics (outer bag and lining), measuring 2½" × 24" (6.4cm × 61cm). (Again, if your fabric is too short, cut two pieces and add a seam to create the 24½" [62.2cm] length. Centering the seam makes for the best results.)

2. ADD INTERFACING

Fuse a super-heavyweight interfacing to the wrong side of one side panel fabric, and a regular fusible interfacing to the other side panel fabric.

Fuse interfacing to the wrong sides of the front panels.

Interface the wrong side of the strap and strap lining using a fusible interfacing. Remember that you're not ironing it on, you're pressing it, so lift and overlap your pressed sections to allow the fusible glue to really heat up and bond to the fabric's wrong side.

STITCH TIP

If you're totally unfamiliar with quilting, you might want to check out the detailed instructions on making a "quilt sandwich" and quilting in the quilting chapters (which starts on page 48).

Quilt the Flap Panel

The quilting on this bag gives it lots of depth and texture. It's also a fun place to start for quilters who don't usually sew bags (and vice versa). But if quilting really isn't your thing, you can totally skip this section if you want. Just cut out two pieces of fabric (one for outer bag, one for lining) to the dimension included in step 1 and move on to the next page.

1. PIN BASTE PANEL, BATTING AND MUSLIN

Layer the flap panel, muslin and backing with muslin on the bottom, then batting, then front panel right-side up on top. Attach the layers with safety pins (called pin basting) spaced about a fist-width apart.

Repeat with the lining fabric—making a whole other quilt sandwich with lining fabric on top.

2. ADD QUILTING STITCHES

Add quilting stitches to the flap. (It's best to sew these stitches with a walking foot.) Stitch lines that are straight but randomly arranged across the body of the panel: vary the direction, the stitch length, the color, whatever you choose to add depth and visual interest.

Repeat with the lining fabric "sandwich." Try a variation here, too, so you get more bang for your buck. Try lots of straight lines very close together, maybe an inch apart. Or try concentric rectangles, echoing the edges of the panel.

Trim the edges of both "quilts."

Create the Side Panels and Front

In this section we'll work on the bag front, not to be confused with the quilted flap, which is the front of the bag that you'll see when the flap is lifted.

The super-heavyweight interfacing you'll use here, which usually is a funny made-up name that ends in "-tex," give shape and support to the bag as a whole by making the side panel super-duper stiff. Combined with the double-quilted front panel, the bag will retain its shape much better than if we'd just used regular interfacing on both sides.

1. STITCH FRONT PANEL TO SIDE PANEL

Place the long side panel right sides together and raw edges even with one front panel. Using a ½" (1.3cm) seam allowance, stitch along three sides, beginning at the upper edge, heading down one side and pivoting at corners. Leave the top edge unstitched.

Repeat this step with the front and side panels for the lining.

2. ATTACH FLAP PANEL TO FRONT/SIDE PANEL

Now you should have two bag fronts-and-sides (shown here). One will be very stiff (the outside of the bag) and the other is the bag lining.

On the opposite side of the side panel (the one with the raw edges), attach the flap panel (which is really a single panel that will be both the back of the bag and the front flap). Attach it just as you did the interior front panel (step 1), but know that you're going to have the "flap" section hanging off the upper edge of the side panel in a way the interior front panel didn't. Be sure to do this with both the outer bag and bag lining.

Repeat with the flap for the lining.

Make the Strap

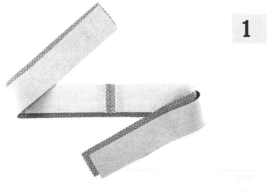

1

1. STITCH STRAP AND LINING TOGETHER
Place the strap and strap lining right sides together. Stitch along both long edges, with a ½" (1.3cm) seam allowance, leaving the short ends open and unstitched.

2. TURN RIGHT-SIDE OUT AND PRESS
Turn right-side out, using a turner as needed. Press aggressively.

2

3. TOPSTITCH
Topstitch along both long edges to secure. If you're feeling kicky, stitch additional rows parallel to the edges through the center of the strap.

3

TIPS FOR TURNING
My all-time preferred method of turning a tube right-side out is to use a bamboo knitting needle—not the pointed end, but the rounded, ball end. Begin turning the tube with your fingers, to get a bit of a "cup" going. Then tuck the ball end of the knitting needle into the cupped portion of the tube. Push gently, using your hands on the ends of the tube to work it right-side out. Bracing the tip of the needle against a table (NOT your lap) will give you some leverage to work the fabric over the needle.

Assemble the Bag

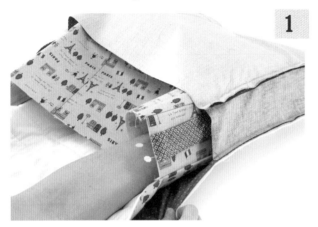

1. PIN BAG AND LINING, TRAPPING STRAPS

Turn the portion that will be the outer bag right-side out. Pin the strap to the side panel at both sides—I recommend using multiple pins here, since these straps like to rotate themselves if they're not firmly anchored. Then slip the entire outer bag, strap included, inside the bag lining. Pin around entire perimeter, including the flap. The strap ought to be trapped between the two bags at this point.

2. BEGIN SEWING TOGETHER; PAUSE AT PIVOT

Begin stitching the bag and lining together (which you'll do around the flap and continuing around the opening of the bag). Start at the center of the flap and pause at the pivot.

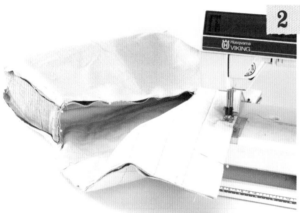

3. CHECK STITCHING AT PIVOT; COMPLETE STITCHING

When you reach the side seams at the bag opening, watch how you handle the pivot. You'll want the seam allowances at the sides to be folded together and push in the same direction. When you do that, you're able to see that the seam allowance where you transition from sewing across the interior front and side panels to the flap lies right on the same ½" (1.3cm) seam line you're about to stitch. It's super important that you line the new stitches up so that they run through the seam as you pivot, to prevent a weird pucker from forming.

Pivot at the join between the flap and the body of the bag to make a clean transition. Continue stitching the rest of the bag, back up to the flap, leaving a gap at the center of the flap through which to turn the bag right-side out.

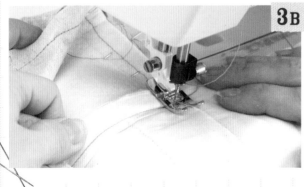

4

4. CLIP INTO PIVOT
Clip into the pivot point at the flap corner, up to the stitching but not through it. Clip the corners of the flap to release the seam allowances.

5. TURN BAG RIGHT-SIDE OUT
Turn the entire bag right-side out by reaching through the opening you left in the flap. Smooth the seams on the interior using a knitting needle. Really push those seams out, especially the quilted ones at the edge of the flap.

6. TOPSTITCH
Press the entire upper edge of bag super firmly. Then topstitch around the entire circumference, catching the seam allowances as you do. You'll want to watch those pivots here, too, and be sure to change direction with the needle in the seam.

5

6

NEXT STEPS

- This narrow, straight-line quilting style is very Japanese in nature, and I'm in love with it everywhere I see it. If you're vibing on the Japanese look, try the **Sashiko Window Treatment** next (see page 42).
- Once you're completely hooked on quilting, you really ought to just bite the bullet and make a whole one. Start with a simple patchwork using the **Paving Stones Quilt** (see page 52).
- Love seeing a different fabric every time you flip open that satchel's flap? Run headlong into the **Tufted Duvet** (see page 30) and choose a different fabric on each side—you'll dream sweet dreams of mixing-and-matching your prints.

LEVEL 4 | CLASSY LADY ELBOW BAG

When I was in eighth grade, my grandmother gave me this spectacular vintage-before-vintage-was-cool handbag, with wooden handles and a button-on cover that could be swapped out when the mood struck. The bag went missing, probably in some forgotten yard sale, but I never forgot how grown-up and classy I felt carrying it. This pattern is inspired by my memory of that bag—thank goodness I no longer have it to compare the two, because the memory is much more satisfying than I suspect real life would be. I'd rather stay classy.

SUPPLIES

½ yd (0.46 m) of cotton fabric for the outer bag

½ yd (0.46 m) of coordinating fabric for the lining

½ yd (0.46 m) of cotton fabric for the bag cover (optional)

½ yd (0.46 m) of coordinating fabric for the cover lining (optional)

Mini-piping, or piping cording plus bias tape to cover it

Matching thread

Six to eight ⅜" (9.5mm) buttons

Cut Fabric and Add Interfacing

1. CUT

Cut two of the bag body from your outer fabric and two from your lining. Repeat with the bag gusset.

Cut the cover from a different fabric, but use the "cut here for cover" cutting line on the pattern piece to shorten the tabs. Repeat for the cover lining fabric.

2. APPLY INTERFACING

Apply fusible interfacing to all six pieces. (If you're using a super stiff fabric or one that already has a lot of body, you can skip the interfacing on the lining only, but still add it to the outer fabric for support and to help the bag hold its shape.)

Create the Bag and Lining

1. PINCH-PRESS AND PIN GUSSET TO ONE BAG SIDE

Pinch-press the gusset to mark the center, and do the same to each side of the bag body. With the right sides of the fabric facing, place the gusset together with one of the bag body. Pin in place. Continue to pin along the edge, keeping the raw edges even as you do. Since the bag body is round and the edge of the gusset it straight, you'll find that the shapes bend a bit as you work; this is how the volume of the bag is built, so go with it!

2. STITCH SIDE TO GUSSET

Stitch, using a ½" (1.3cm) seam allowance, from the center to the end of the gusset in one direction, and then from the center to the end of the gusset in the other direction.

3. SEW ON OTHER SIDE

Pin the other side in place and stitch that as well. Clip all the curves.

Repeat steps 2–3 with the lining.

Attach the Outer Bag and Lining

1. PIN OUTER BAG TO LINING

Turn the outer bag right-side out. Place it fully inside the lining, and pin around the upper edge, making sure to match up the seams.

2. STITCH

Stitch around the upper edge, beginning along the straight handle tab on one side. As you arrive at each corner seam, stop with the needle IN the seam and pivot to work your way around the side of the bag—it makes all the difference in the world if, as you're sewing, the seam you're putting in lines right up with the seams that are already there.

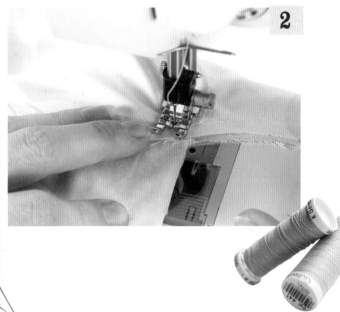

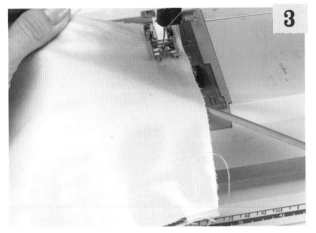

3. LEAVE OPENING ALONG TAB

When you get all the way around, STOP sewing about three inches BEFORE where you began, leaving an opening in one of the tabs.

4. CLIP CORNERS

Clip into the corners, up to the stitching but not through it.

5. TURN, PRESS AND TOPSTITCH

Turn the whole thing right-side out by reaching into the opening you left in the tab and teasing out the fabric until the whole bag spills out and you're able to stuff the lining back inside. Press aggressively, getting those upper edges nice and flat so you can add the handles next. Topstitch the opening closed.

Add the Buttons and Finish

To attach the cover (which you'll make in the next section) you want buttons to which that new cover can attach. Begin with any small button, but best is one 3/8" (9.5mm) in diameter. These can be decorative, covered, standard, mismatched, your choice. You'll need three buttons. (If you've decided against making a cover, skip to step 2.)

1. STITCH BUTTONS ON MAIN BAG

On the main bag, mark the placement of the three buttons using the marks on the pattern as a guide. Sew them on either by hand or machine. These buttons will hold only the weight of the cover, not of the contents of the bag, so you don't need them to be super snugly stitched.

2. STITCH TAB CLOSED AROUND HANDLE

With the bag right-side out, place one handle on one tab, on the lining side. Fold the tab to the inside, encasing the handle within it. Use four strands of regular thread or two of embroidery floss to hand-stitch the handle in place using a whipstitch. Yes, by hand—it would be a neat trick to get this under the machine! (See the Crash Course on hand-stitches below as needed.) Repeat on the opposite side with the other handle.

Test the strength of your handles by placing your wallet, cell phone, etc., inside and swing it wildly. If you've stitched well, you'll see that the threads remain firm and in place; if you notice any movement now, you'll want to go back and re-sew.

CRASH COURSE: HAND-STITCHES

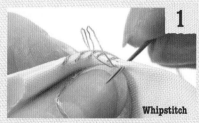

Whipstitch

Slipstitch

Ladder Stitch

Place the tip of your needle in the fabric on the right, then push through and pull the thread to the opposite side. Cross the needle back over to the right and stitch again, making little loops over the edge to be stitched as you do. A strong stitch.

Place the needle in the fabric just at the fold line. Cross over to the other side, pick up a few stitches of the opposite fold and pull through. Continue bouncing back and forth, picking up only a few threads each time. Creates an invisible closure.

Similar to the slipstitch, the ladder stitch asks you to place the needle in the fold of the fabric, pull through and then skip across, making "bars" between the two edges to be joined. Another nearly invisible stitch.

Make the Cover

Here's where we make the interchangeable cover to this bag, which fits over the entire exterior of the bag and changes its appearance. Wouldn't it be fun to do one of these covers in sequins? Or how about an embroidered one? I love that the versatility of this bag is that you can make a simple, everyday bag and then attach a more dressy or punchy outer cover, and you'll have a WHOLE NEW BAG without having to even take out your wallet—two bags for the price of one. (You totally don't have to make a cover if one bag for the price of one is good enough for you.)

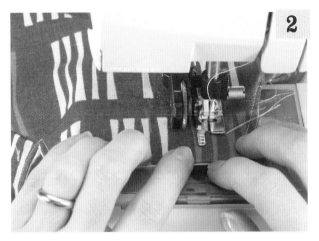

1. SEW THE COVER AND LINING

Sew the cover as you did for the main bag (pages 119–121), then repeat to make the cover lining.

2. STITCH BUTTONHOLES ON COVER

After pressing the tabs nice and smooth and topstitching (step 5, page 121), mark the placement of the buttonholes. You'll want these to line up perfectly with the buttons you installed on the bag, so go ahead and slip the bag inside the cover to mark where the buttonholes belong.

Stitch those buttonholes in place. (If needed, check out the Crash Course for stitching buttonholes on page 169 in the Sewing for Children chapter.)

NEXT STEPS

The buttons here call to mind the **Tufted Duvet** (see page 30) with its covered buttons and simple closure. Try that project to perfect your buttonhole-making skills and work on making covered buttons to spice up any project!

Making a bag is sometimes about completing an outfit. Move on to the **Enchantment Under the Sea Dress** (see page 188)—when worn with this bag, it's a trip to a retro wonderland!

LEVEL 5 | BEADED EVENING CLUTCH

I love to go on dates with my husband: a night out without the kids, someplace where they have cloth napkins and no one is screaming for more ketchup. It's pretty magical. And I refuse, under all circumstances, to carry my Mom Bag with me—no receipts falling out, no embarrassing stray fish crackers, no sippy cups spilling just before we get to the main course. Something chic and clean, something just a little bit sparkly and delicate. This metal-frame clutch is the perfect solution: just enough room for only the essentials, a slightly puffed body for easy carrying and just the right number of beads to up the WOW factor.

SUPPLIES

½ yd (0.46 m) of delicious fabric you might not otherwise splurge on, like silk or imported cotton

½ yd (0.46 m) of super heavy-weight interfacing

½ yd (0.46 m) of coordinating fabric for the lining

Matching thread

Small glass beads (optional), along with transparent nylon thread

Hand-sewing needle

Beading

Believe it or not, the beading really does have to be done now so that the stitches attaching the beads and stones don't show on the interior of the bag later. I only beaded the front of my bag, but you can certainly bead both sides. Doing only one side can be very chic and less likely to snag on fancy dress clothes; doing both makes the bag fully reversible and can look exceedingly expensive (even though it really wasn't!). And if beading and embellishment is really not your thing, you're perfectly welcome to skip this step entirely and get right to sewing.

1

1. TRANSFER SHAPE TO FABRIC; DON'T CUT

Using the template, transfer the shape of the bag front onto the piece of fabric you're using for the front of the purse. DO NOT cut the fabric yet.

2. LAY OUT BEADS USING TEMPLATE

Lay out your beads and stones on the fabric with the drawn-in edge of the bag front as your guide. (Be sure to give yourself that ½" [1.3cm] seam allowance on all sides as you work, so you're not beading in a place where they won't be seen!) I recommend taking a digital photo of the arrangement before you remove the beads and begin to work. If you enlarge it on your computer screen, it will give you a visual reference to use as you attach the beads, eliminating guesswork. I went with a starburst motif, but you can create any design that conveys your elegance.

3

3. HAND-STITCH ON BEADS

Place the fabric in an embroidery hoop to hold it taut as you work. If you have a particularly fine fabric or one that isn't super strong, include a layer of tear-away or spray-away stabilizer in the hoop to help support the fabric as you attach the beads.

Using two thicknesses of polyester thread, begin sewing the beads in place. For larger beads and stones, sew each one separately to really anchor them down; for smaller beads or beads that are more closely spaced, sew in sequence using a backstitch.

Repeat with the opposite side, if desired.

Prepare the Clutch Body

Before you cut, let's talk textiles. For this clutch, you'll choose a fabric for the outside (probably silk or some other evening-y fabric) and also a fabric for the lining, which you can totally have fun with. Imagine: You're on a blind date, it isn't going very well, you peek into your bag, suddenly things are much brighter!

You'll also need regular interfacing for the lining and ultra-heavy-weight interfacing, like Peltex, for the outside of the bag. I strongly recommend the sew-in type of heavy-weight interfacing for silks; it's less likely to show puckers. Super stiff interfacing makes the bag pop up and sit on its own, even when empty. You can use a slightly less stiff interfacing, but the clutch frame is pretty heavy, so you'll need at least a heavyweight interfacing just to hold it up without collapsing.

1

1. CUT FABRIC AND INTERFACE; MARK

Cut the beaded section out of the fabric, and remove the stabilizer if you used any. Cut another of the purse body of your main fabric, and two of the lining.

Cut two of the purse body of heavy-weight interfacing (like Peltex) and two of fusible interfacing. Apply the fusible interfacing to the wrong side of both lining pieces. Attach the ultra-heavy-weight fusible interfacing to both pieces of the main fabric. Do this either by basting ¼" (6.4mm) from the raw edge on all sides or by fusing (depending on your type of interfacing).

Using the pattern as your guide, transfer the marks for the clutch opening to the wrong side of the fabric.

2

2. STITCH FROM DOT TO DOT

Place the two front bag pieces right sides together. Stitch from one dot to the other along the sides and bottom of the bag, changing direction with a slight pivot at the pointed lower edge. Repeat with lining, but this time leave an opening (to turn it all right-side out later).

Trim your seam allowances to about ¼" (6.4mm) and clip corners.

TIPS FOR WORKING WITH SILKS

Silk is an exceptionally strong fiber and can behave differently beneath your needle than cottons. A few tips will help you master this fine natural fiber and make something lovely!

1. Use a new, smaller machine needle. A sharper needle will pierce silk better than an old, dull one.
2. Use pins specially made for silk—they're narrower and sharper, and less likely to leave gaping holes in your fabric.
3. If your silk is especially slippery, try using a walking foot to stabilize the fabric.
4. Silk can fray like crazy—consider cutting with pinking shears to limit this.
5. When pressing silk, you can often see lumps and puckers. Start by pressing both sides flat, to set the stitches. Then press your seam allowances open to get a smooth finish!

3. TURN OUTER BAG AND PUT IN LINING

Turn the outer bag right-side out. If your interfacing resists at this stage, be patient and gentle, and tease it on out. You'll sacrifice a few extra minutes here, but the results will last longer and be completely worth it. Place the lining (which is still inside out) over the entire outer bag, with right sides together, matching all seams.

4. STITCH UPPER EDGE

Stitch the upper edge of the bag by placing it under the needle, sewing one flap through all thicknesses from one side seam to the opposite side seam. Backstitch at both ends. DO NOT stitch across the side seam. Instead, do each flap separately, beginning and ending each seam at the side seam.

5. CLIP CURVES AND TRIM SEAM ALLOWANCES

Clip the curved upper edge to allow it to turn right-side out neatly, and trim the seam allowances ¼" (6.4mm) or so with knife-edge appliqué scissors or any other super sharp blade.

6. SEW OPENING SHUT

Wrestle the outer bag through the opening so that bag is right-side out. Press aggressively to make a nice, smooth edge at the flap where it will attach to the frame—if you're using silk or another delicate fabric, do this pressing from the inside. Press with lots of steam, which will help the Peltex mold to the shapes you need.

Then stitch across the opening you left, very close to the edge.

STITCH TIP

When pressing a bag with lining, I like to "cheat" the seam a little to the interior so I don't see any of the lining from outside the bag. Do this by slightly "rolling" the seam over as you press, so the stitches are ever-so-slightly tipped toward the inside of the bag.

Attach the Metal Frame

There are two types of metal clutch frames: sew-in and groove. Instructions for both are below.

Groove Frame

1. PUT GLUE ON ONE FRAME SIDE

Using a high-strength fabric glue, squeeze a generous amount across the groove on only one side of the frame. Set it aside and allow it to get tacky (about five minutes). Repeat on only one flap edge of the bag.

2. EASE BAG EDGE INTO FRAME

When the glue is sufficiently set, begin placing the glued-up bag edge into the glued frame edge, starting at the hinge. Gently ease the edge as far into the groove as you're able, continuing along the opening until the entire side is secured. Flip the bag over and be sure you've also caught the lining side neatly. It doesn't matter a ton if you get some glue on the frame, but do take care not to get it on the fabric—it won't come out! This will seem hopeless and impossible at first, because the stiffness of the bag is really resistant—have faith!

3. REPEAT ON OTHER SIDE

Allow the bag to set up for fifteen minutes. Now move on to the other side using the same steps. Leave the frame overnight to cure before using.

Note: *Some folks squeeze this type of frame with pliers to hold the bag, in lieu of glue. That's an okay idea, but be careful to squeeze hard enough to give the frame the strength it needs, and to use your pliers in regular intervals to make a neat appearance.*

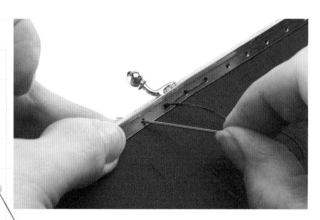

Sew-In Frame

As with the glue-in frame (step 2, above), place the bag edge into the frame edge. Once the edge is lined up with the frame, sew through the holes at the edge of the frame, securing it to the edge of the bag using a backstitch and four thicknesses of thread.

TRY THIS, TOO!

Using a cotton or wool for this same clutch makes a really snazzy daytime version! Leave out the beading and you've got the perfect bag for heading to a meeting with the principal, say, or maybe even meeting your husband for drinks afterward.

NEXT STEPS

Like adding a little glue to your sewing to break you out of a rut? Skip back to the **Photo-Transfer Wall Art** (see page 36) and use your glue to give shape and structure to some really cool sewing.

Hand-beading any project gives it a truly one-of-a-kind feel that can't be beat. Check out the **Knit Top** (see page 172) with its beaded variation, and see how it can take your wardrobe to fabulous with just a few well-placed stitches.

It's a short step from using your hand-beading skills to doing hand-quilting. Take your next step on the **Whole Cloth Quilt** (see page 84) and see how quickly you can transform the most basic of supplies into something truly showstopping.

SECTION 4:
SEWING FOR CHILDREN

When I was little, my mom sewed for me and my sister. Sometimes we'd get matching outfits—all three of us. It was the 70s, you know how it goes. And as ridiculous as it sounded to middle-school-me, now I look back and those matching-outfit days hold some of my dearest memories. Now that I have children of my own, I love making them things at my machine that build memories and bring all of us joy. And when they come to me to request something special sewn on my machine? Well, it just doesn't get much better than that.

LEVEL 1 | REVERSIBLE GIRL'S DRESS

I came up with this dress when my daughters were itty bitties. I was so bummed every time they out-grew something I'd made with hoarded fabric—once they were too big to wear it, I was forced to pack it away and lost the chance to look at the prints I love so much! Step one: Make it reversible, so I can use two fabrics at the same time (and so we always have a spare outfit near at hand for random food incidents). Step two: Make it adjustable with tie straps that really tie, so the dress can be raised and lowered at the underarm as she grows, giving her the chance to wear it as a dress to start, as a tunic later and as a swing top before it gets retired. I'm all about making the good stuff last just a little bit longer.

SUPPLIES

1-1¾ yd (0.91-1.6 m) cotton fabric for the dress

1-1¾ yd (0.91-1.6 m) cotton fabric for the lining/reverse

Matching thread

Cut the Pattern

This dress is a very simple one, but its success hinges largely on good cutting.

1. ARRANGE PATTERN ON FABRICS

Fold both your fabrics in half (as shown). Lay the pattern pieces on top (being sure to match the fold line on the pattern with the folds on the fabric) and cut them out.

I like to lay out one fabric, then lay the other directly on top of it, and cut both the outer dress and the lining/reverse at the same time. For the largest size of this pattern, you won't be able to fit the pattern on with the fabric folded this way; instead, fold the fabric with selvages together and cut each piece on the fold.

2. CUT CURVES CAREFULLY

The curves at the straps are pretty tight, so when you reach them, take care cutting them out to preserve as much of them as you can. Consider using super small scissors to do just this one section of cutting.

3. PIN OUTER DRESS AND LINING

Place the lining and outer dresses right sides together, matching side seams, notches and keeping raw edges even. Pin to secure all the way around the upper edge, including the straps and curved neckline. Use plenty of pins if you need to—remember, pins are not about rules; pins are about confidence, and you ought to use as many or as few as you need to make you feel good about the results you'll get.

4. STITCH TOGETHER

Stitch all the way around the upper edge, including the front and back necklines and the straps. Do not stitch the bottom hem (this is how you'll turn the dress right-side out later).

Take care to stitch slowly on the curves—if they're really giving you a tough time, try shortening your stitch length to allow you a little more control as you round those strap ends. A sketchy or jagged seam here will show right at the top of the garment where it's the most obvious, so if I were going to rush through any part of this project, here would not be the place. Take your time with the straps and they will reward you!

5. CLIP CURVES AND TRIM SEAM ALLOWANCE

Clip the curves on the neckline seam allowance (up to but not through the stitches). Trim the seam allowance on each strap to a scant ¼" (6.4mm). This will keep the curves nice and defined as you flip the dress right-side out—if you turn the whole thing and find a big lumpy blob, go back and make more clips closer together and trim just a bit more.

6. TURN RIGHT-SIDE OUT AND PRESS

Turn right-side out through the open hem, using a knitting needle to get really clean curves on the strap ends. Press, press, press. Use steam. Force those straps into submission.

Hem a Reversible

The hem is the real key in keeping this dress totally reversible: no part of the fabric from one side can peek below the hemline on the other. This dress doesn't have to be truly reversible—if you want, the reverse side can simply be a lining. But really, why line it when you can just get two dresses for the work it takes to make one?

1. PRESS LOWER EDGES UNDER

Begin by pulling the lining away from the outer dress, and pressing under ½" (1.3cm) on the lower edge of the outer dress. Do the same on the lower edge of the lining.

2. PIN HEMLINE IN PLACE

Place the two folded edges together at the hemline. At the side seams, give a gentle tug to make sure there is no slack, then pin at the lower edge, taking care to keep the two folded edges even. Forcing them to be even when they aren't pressed to the same depth will make puckers and bulges in the rest of the dress, so take care with this step—it will make all the difference in the end.

Continue in this manner all the way around the hemline, and re-press any edges that want to escape your rigorous checking. Pin the edges in place.

3. STITCH THE HEM

After the entire hemline is pinned, stitch the hem ¼" (6.4mm) from the lower edge.

4. TOPSTITCH NECKLINE AND STRAPS

In the same way that you hemmed the lower edge, let's topstitch around the upper edge. Sew ¼" (6.4mm) from the edge all the way around the neckline and straps, backstitching when you return to where you began. Not only does this secure the seam allowances on the inside of the dress and keep them from getting lumpy when we launder it, topstitching here will keep the look of the garment consistent. (When you reach the straps, you might need to get closer to the edges than ¼" (6.4mm)—this is totally fine, just be consistent!)

Tie the Straps

TIE STRAPS

To hold the dress up, tie knots. To make the best knot, one that will lie flat when tied and not rotate around, tie the knot first with right tie over left, then the second knot with left over right. This will help your "ears" to point straight!

NEXT STEPS

Nothing gets me happier at my machine than making something reversible. Try the **Reversible Quilted Satchel** next (see page 112) and embrace my passion for all things multi-functional.

I never thought I was a matchy-matchy kind of girl, but when you sew, you can get as quirky as you like. After making this dress, try the **Enchantment Under the Sea Dress** (see page 188) for you—in a matching fabric (or not).

Did you love adding the rickrack trim in the variation? Try the **Ribboned Envelope Pillow** (see page 16) and continue your love affair with trim.

TRY THIS, TOO!

One of my favorite ways to mix this dress up is to simply catch a little rickrack in the hemline as I stitch it. You'll see the waves of the trim peeking out at the lower edge of the dress on both sides, so choose a color that works with both your fabrics. Consider using appliqué, embroidery or pockets on one or both sides to spice up versions of this dress—no kidding, my girls wear them all year long, over almost anything, and I can't get enough of them in their closets.

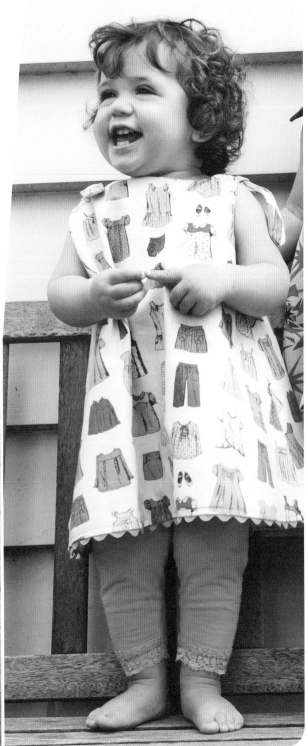

LEVEL 2 | LOVIE BLANKET

Make this super sweet animal friend with attached lovie blanket from any soft fabric, like flannel or minky. Minky is a specialty fabric that is made from polyester—normally, I refuse to work with polyester, but in this case it's a soft, furlike fiber that kids really adore. And really, sewing for children is all about making them something that they can love on until it becomes Real. What a tremendous gift your sewing machine can give!

SUPPLIES

½ yd (0.46 m) of minky or fuzzy or fluffy fabric

1 fat quarter of fabric for lining

Matching thread

Polyfill stuffing

Embroidery floss and needle for eyes and nose

Choose the Fabric and Cut

Any soft fabric will do for this lovie, but to make it extra soft and special, I recommend minky. Be prepared in advance for the surreal amount of shedding that minky produces. When you complete a project with minky, be sure to clean and oil your machine to get rid of all those little fly-aways. For the lining, use a satiny fabric for a cool, smooth touch or a cotton for washability—your choice.

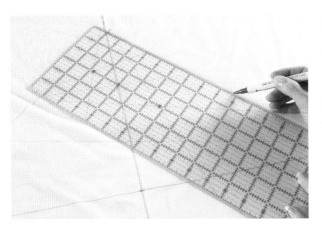

CUT FABRIC

We need two triangles to make the body of this sweet little fella, so let's begin by cutting a square, which we'll divide along a diagonal into two triangles. On your main fabric, mark a square that's 18" × 18" (45.7cm × 45.7cm). Then mark lines that go directly across the center from point to point in both directions, so you have a T-shape down the middle of the square. Cut out the square. Then cut the square in half along the diagonal you marked. These two triangular panels will form the body of the blanket.

Cut one head gusset of main fabric. Cut two ears of main fabric and two ear linings of lining fabric. (You'll cut the body lining fabric later.)

Stitch the Ears, Head and Body

Curved seams are more than just fun to look at—they're the perfect way to add volume, or in this case, to make a three-dimensional shape with your fabric. By adding curved seams to the head of this lovie, we're allowing for stuffing to fill out a rounded shape by putting volume in where it wasn't before.

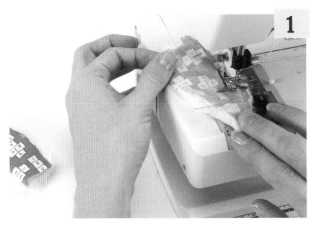

1. STITCH EAR AND EAR LINING

Place the ear lining and ear right sides together and stitch from base to point, using a ⅜" (9.5mm) seam allowance. Repeat with the other ear. Turn both right-side out.

STITCH TIP

After turning your ears right-side out, check the seamline to see if any of the "hairs" have been trapped—if they have, use the tip of your seam ripper to very gently tease them loose.

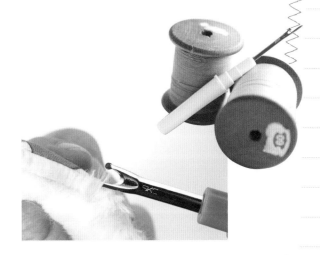

2. PINCH EARS AND BASTE

Take one ear piece and pinch the lower edge to form a crease; baste that pinch in place. Repeat with the other ear.

3. PLACE EAR ON HEAD GUSSET

Lay the ear on the head gusset, with raw edges even. Pin in place, taking care with the angle of the ear—how it is stitched in now will affect the angle it has later, so if you want an animal with attitude, make it so.

4. SEW HEAD GUSSET, EAR AND SIDE PANEL

Place the head gusset and side panel right sides together, matching small and large dots, and catching the ear between them. Sew a generous ⅜" (9.5mm) seam allowance from dot to dot, backstitching at each dot. For more tips on working with faux fur or hairy fabrics, see the sidebar below.

5. REPEAT WITH THE OTHER SIDE

Repeat steps 3 and 4 with the other pieces.

6. BACKSTITCH

From the large dot, backstitch. Now attach the second side panel and ear to the gusset as you did the first one. You'll see the head beginning to take shape now!

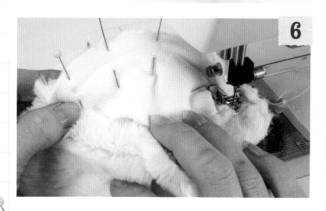

WORKING WITH FAUX FUR

The trick to working with fabrics like minky and faux fur is the pile. As you sew, you'll notice that the pile gets caught frequently under the needle and can be trapped lying flat rather than popping up. As you complete a seam, take your seam ripper and go back to free these trapped fibers.

Pile can also make the fabrics shift as you're sewing them, and many folks find that using a walking foot can ameliorate this issue and make the fabric move more securely through the machine, without bunching or sliding. You might also find LOTS of pins are helpful—as close together as one inch, if you need them.

Finally, when you're sewing minky to another fabric, working with the minky side down toward the feed dogs can help prevent puckering.

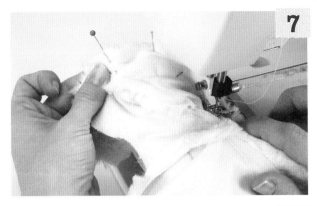

7. COMPLETE SEAM ON HEAD

Complete the seam down the back side of the head (made up of the combined side panel and gusset). Backstitch to form the neck

8. STITCH SEAM TO LOWER EDGE

Stitch down to the lower edge of the blanket. Repeat from the small dot to the edge of the blanket.

Clip all the curved seams, taking care not to snip through the stitching. Turn right-side out. You should now have a square blanket with a head sticking out of the top. Awesome.

Stuffing the Head

Stuffing is almost always done with some form of polyester fiberfill. The softness of this type of stuffing really can't be beat, and it gives the appropriate dimension and shape to your little friend's noggin.

STUFF HEAD

Turn the blanket upside down so you can access the opening at the base of the head. Stuff the head firmly (or loosely, as you prefer) with polyfill. Get into all the little nooks. It can be helpful to use the knob end of a wooden knitting needle for this step.

Flip back over and check your work, taking care not to dislodge the stuffing as you do.

TIPS FOR WORKING WITH FIBERFILL

Let me tell you the secret trick to working with fiberfill: small bites. It's true! We're all tempted to stick our hands into the bag of fluff and grab as much as we can, then stuff it into our project. But when you use large handfuls, the chunks you grabbed together tend to bind to one another, so big handfuls become big blobs. If you take teeny pinches, on the other hand, and put them in a little bit at a time, as those fibers are agitated they'll bind with the other teeny bits next to them, making a cohesive pillow on the inside. Stuffing with fluff is TV work and should be done a little pinch at a time!

Add the Lining

1. CUT LINING FABRIC

With the head firmly attached, but the neck still open and stuffed, lay the lovie flat on the wrong side of your lining fabric. Cut around the edge of the lovie to make a lining that's the same size.

2. STITCH LINING TO BLANKET, LEAVING HOLE

Place the lining and blanket right sides together, trapping the stuffed head between them, and stitch around all four sides, leaving a 4" (10.2cm) opening to turn.

3. TURN AND TOPSTITCH

Clip each of the four corners to reduce the bulk there. Turn right-side out. Press from the lining side to make a clean, crisp edge, then topstitch all the way around all four sides, catching the opening closed as you do.

4. STITCH AROUND HEAD BASE

Place the blanket head-side up in front of you. With all the edges neatly aligned, stitch in a circle around the base of the head to secure the stuffing.

Hand-Stitch the Face

1. HAND-STITCH NOSE

Using pink embroidery thread, add the nose. Using a satin stitch, simply place the needle under the fabric and bring it back around as you create depth and good coverage.

2. HAND-STITCH EYES

Using blue (or your choice of) embroidery thread and satin stitch, add the eyes.

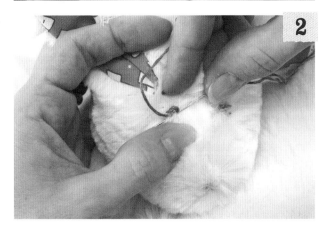

Part of the challenge of this project is working with fabrics that might not be familiar to you. Move to the next stage with the **Beaded Evening Clutch** (see page 124) in a lovely silk, and see how great it can be to break outside of cotton.

The stuffing used here is the same that's used in the **Improvisational Landscape Wall Quilt** (see page 90) to make the three-dimensional trapunto effect. Move to that project next to see how adding more dimension to your projects gives you more options.

NEXT STEPS

LEVEL 3 | TRAVEL MATCHING GAME

Most of the time, when we sew, it's things for the home or clothes to wear. Even toys usually get lumped into stuffed animals, and the fun ends there. Well, no longer for you, little one. This fantastic matching game allows you to choose just the bestest bits of your favorite fabrics and put them together into a simple patchwork where they'll be enjoyed over and over again. And because the project is designed with interchangeable inserts, you can mix it up every time the kids get bored!

SUPPLIES

Scraps of fabric with interesting designs, graphics, novelty images or colors

1½ yds (1.37 m) of home-dec weight fabric for the body of the game

½ yd (0.46m) of Peltex

½ yd (0.46m) of muslin for gameboard backing

Matching thread

Hooks and eyes or snaps

Fussy Cutting

The term "fussy cutting" refers to cutting a fabric specifically to showcase a particular part of the print, which will then be centered or featured in a stitched design. For this project, those fussy-cut squares will be the images to be matched when the game is played.

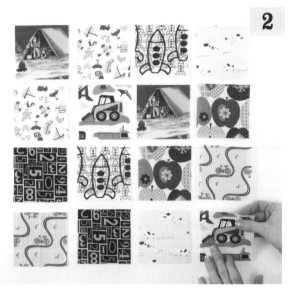

1. CUT FABRIC SQUARES

Choose eight prints you really love, each with an image or design that measures at least 1" (2.5cm) across, and that contains two of this same image. Cut sixteen squares—two each of the eight prints—measuring 3¼" × 3¼" (9.5cm × 9.5cm). Center the element of your print that you want to highlight before you cut.

2. ARRANGE SQUARES

Arrange the squares on a flat surface, mixing them up until you're satisfied with the placement. You probably want to avoid having too many of the same print side by side, but it's a game, so it might not matter that much.

Make the Matching Card Insert

To make the front of the cards, you'll basically be making a patchwork. When you're finished, you'll add ultra-heavy-weight interfacing, which serves to stiffen the board so it can slide in and out of the memory game, and be exchanged for other boards—nonstop fun!

1. STITCH ROWS

Beginning at the upper-left corner, place the first square right sides together with the second square, and stitch a ¼" (6.4mm) seam. Continue along until every square in the row has been stitched, creating a long strip of squares.

    Press the seam allowances together and to one side.

    Repeat this step with the other three rows.

2. SEW ROWS TOGETHER

Take the top row, place it right sides together with the row beneath it and match the seams. Pin in place, then stitch a ¼" (6.4mm) seam across the rows to join them. Take the next row, place it right sides together with the second row and repeat. Continue until all four rows are joined into one large square piece of patchwork.

    Press the seam allowances open.

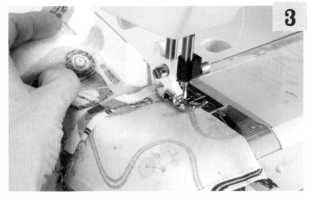

3. STITCH CARD TO BACKING

Cut one piece of your backing fabric measuring 14½" × 14½" (36.8cm × 36.8cm). Place it right sides together with the patchwork memory card. Stitch a ¼" (6.4mm) seam allowance around all four sides, leaving an opening about 6" (15.2cm) wide. Backstitch around the opening and pivot at the corners.

Clip the corners to remove bulk so you'll have nice, square points.

4. ADD INTERFACING

Turn the card right-side out. Press aggressively. Cut a piece of ultra-heavy-weight interfacing like Peltex measuring 14" × 14" (35.6cm × 35.6cm). Insert it through the opening, making sure the corners reach the very edges of the board. Topstitch it shut.

Add Windows to the Board Front

1. MARK WINDOWS

Cut three pieces of your board fabric—a home dec weight is best—measuring 15" × 15" (38.1cm × 38.1cm). Set two pieces aside. Take the third piece and on it, mark (chalk, pencil or ink) four rows of four squares each, with squares measuring 2¾" × 2¾" (7cm × 7cm). To keep things centered and even, begin by marking—lightly—the exact center of the fabric. Then, mark ¼" (6.4mm) on either side of that, from top to bottom. From those lines, measure 2¾" (7cm) to make one row, which can then be divided up into squares. Continue until you have four rows of four squares each.

2. ADD MUSLIN AND STITCH MARKED LINES

Trim a piece of muslin or solid cotton to fit the edges of the board fabric—no need to be exact. Place that right sides together with the board fabric. Press it to keep it neat and smooth—pin in place, if necessary. On each and every square, stitch directly on top of the lines to create stitched boxes—all the way around all four sides, leaving no opening and pivoting at the corners. Trim all excess threads.

3. MAKE DIAGONAL CUTS

In the center of each box, clip into the fabric at the heart of the square (it doesn't matter which fabric is facing up). Make two diagonal cuts (that form an X) across the square, each from one corner to the other. Trim through both layers. When you're finished you'll have four triangular flaps of fabric.

4. CUT OUT SQUARE

Now cut out the square so there is a scant ¼" (6.4mm) seam allowance around the seam (again, doesn't matter which fabric is facing up—I turned mine to the muslin side, just so the cuts are easier to see in the photo). When you're finished, instead of four triangles, you'll have four tabs of fabric and the square will be open.

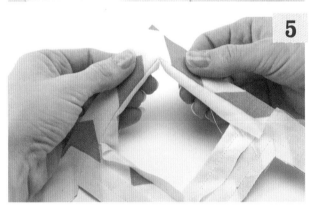

5. FLIP MUSLIN THROUGH OPENING

Now you should be able to flip the solid cotton/muslin through the opening and around to the wrong side of the printed fabric, creating a window with clean, crisp edges. Press, press, press until each window agrees to lie flat. Trim any excess fabric that might peek through a window, but leave no less than ¼" (6.4mm) around each opening.

6. TOPSTITCH

On the right side of the printed fabric, topstitch the flaps in place by sewing around each opening in a square, pivoting at the corners.

Make the Window Covers and Add Snaps

1. CUT AND STITCH SQUARES TOGETHER; TOPSTITCH

Cut thirty-two squares of the board fabric, each measuring 4" × 4" (10.2cm × 10.2cm). (See the note below about hook-and-loop closures.) Place two squares right sides together and stitch around all four sides, leaving an opening to turn. Clip the corners. Turn right-side out and press into submission. Topstitch all four sides of the square, catching the opening shut as you do.

Repeat this process for all thirty-two pieces to make a total of sixteen double-sided squares.

2. INSTALL SNAPS

Using a snap press or pliers, install a male snap at the upper center of each opening on the board front. Install the matching female snap on the upper center of one window covering. Repeat to attach snaps to all sixteen windows and all sixteen coverings.

Note: If you prefer, you can use hook-and-loop closures (like Velcro) instead of snaps. Stitch the hook-and-loop tape on the front of the window covers before assembling the squares.

Stitch the Board Back and Assemble the Game

1. STITCH BOARD BACK; ADD INTERFACING

Place the other two right sides together and stitch a ¼" (6.4mm) seam all the way around all four sides, leaving an opening to turn. Clip the corners at a diagonal. Turn right-side out and press aggressively, keeping edges nice and neat and corners crisp. Set aside. Insert Peltex, turn and topstitch (as you did with the memory card).

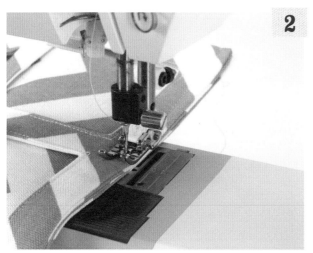

2. STITCH WINDOW PANEL TO BOARD BACK

With the flaps removed, place the window panel right-side up on top of the board back, which should be front-side up. Stitch a narrow topstitched seam around the two sides and bottom, leaving the top edge unstitched to allow an opening for the memory card to slide in.

3. ASSEMBLE THE GAME

To assemble the game, simply slip the matching board in between the peekaboo panel and the backing board to play. Reattach the window coverings. Make multiple memory boards for multiple games!

Cutting little squares apart and putting them back together doesn't sound like art, but you've found through this project that such a simple skill can have powerful results. Explore that some more by moving on to the **Paving Stones Quilt** (see page 52) and working with color and shape in patchwork.

The windows you made here required one method of manipulating fabric to make an opening—try another method with the **A-Line Skirt** (see page 180), and see how you can give a glimpse into another fabric through a simple vented opening.

Take your memory game for a trip in your **Fabric Picnic Basket** (see page 106), and make some new memories to share!

NEXT STEPS

LEVEL 4 | LAY-FLAT BACKPACK

My kids have lots and lots (and LOTS) of bags and buckets and carryalls for toting their treasures around, along with anything else they can find and fit inside. But as each of them has moved through preschool and on to Big Kid School—the kind with homework and notes from the teacher, giant round pencils with nubby erasers, stickers and juice time—I have found that they need a bit more of a backpack to hold it all. This one gives them little pockets for the little things, but also unzips all the way flat to allow total access—and to discourage small hands from filling it up super full. Working with a two-way zip will change the way you think about the possibilities of closures!

SUPPLIES

1½ yds (1.37 m) of home dec cotton or cotton/linen midweight fabric

1 yd (0.91 m) of lining fabric

½ yd (0.46 m) of Peltex

1 set of backpack hardware with sliders

Matching thread

½ yd (0.46 m) of lining fabric made into 2" (5 cm) single-fold bias tape

Cut and Interface

1. CUT BACKPACK PIECES

Cut the zipper panel to measure 35" × 5" (88.9cm × 12.7cm). Now cut it in half lengthwise, so you have two pieces that measure 35" × 2½" (88.9cm × 6.4cm).

Cut your main pocket and the pencil holder, one piece of fabric and one of lining measuring 6" × 13" (15.2cm × 33cm) for the pocket and one piece of fabric plus one piece of lining measuring 4½" × 16" (11.4cm × 40.6cm) for the pencil holder.

Cut the bottom panel in the main fabric to 11" × 4½" (27.9cm × 11.4cm). Cut your bottom panel lining fabric to the same size.

Cut the front and back panels from your main fabric; they should measure 13" × 10" (33cm × 25.4cm) each. Cut two pieces of lining fabric to 13" × 10" (33cm × 25.4cm). And cut two pieces of ultra-heavy-duty interfacing to 13" × 10" (33cm × 25.4cm).

Cut the straps: two pieces that measure 22" × 4½" (55.9cm × 11.4cm).

2. APPLY INTERFACING

Cut two pieces of super-heavyweight interfacing that measure 35" × 1½" (88.9cm × 3.8cm). Fuse these to the wrong sides of the zipper panel halves, centering them so that ½" (1.3cm) on either side of the interfacing remains free—this is where you'll put your seams, and subtracting the interfacing will remove bulk.

Create the main pocket by applying interfacing to the wrong side of the main fabric.

Baste or fuse the interfacing to the wrong side of the front and back panel (in the main fabric).

Baste or fuse the interfacing to the wrong side of the bottom panel (in the lining fabric).

Make the Zipper Panel

The zipper panel creates the sides, top and part of the bottom of the bag. By making this into all one piece, we create a "frame" for the body of the bag to fit into. And speaking of zippers, be sure it's a TWO-WAY zip.

1. FOLD EDGES OF ZIPPER PANEL HALVES

Press under one long edge on each side of the zipper panel ¼" (6.4mm). These two edges will face one another with the zipper teeth between them in the finished bag.

2. STITCH ZIPPER TO PANEL

Lay the two-way zipper face up on your work surface, then place one zipper panel's folded edge on top, right-side up, lining the fold up next to the zipper teeth. Using your zipper foot, stitch along the edge of the zipper teeth to secure through all layers, keeping the folded edge of the zipper panel right close to the zipper teeth the whole time.

Repeat on the opposite side, taking care that the raw ends of the center panel pieces line up nice and square once the zipper is installed.

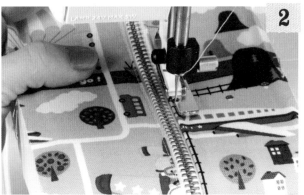

3. CHECK ZIPPER

Pull the zipper closed to check the fit—if the zipper won't slide, double-check that you haven't stitched over the teeth or stitched too close to them to allow the pull to pass by correctly.

Stitch the Pockets and Pencil Holder

Create a main pocket and then create a pencil holder by making another, similar pocket that you'll then use to create pencil loops.

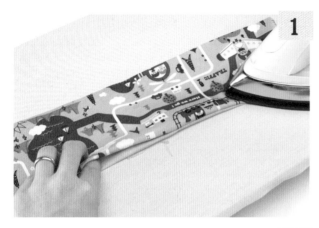

1. STITCH POCKET PIECE

Place the main pocket (in the main fabric) right sides together with the lining. Stitch all four sides, leaving an opening. Turn right-side out, press edge crisply, then topstitch along that upper edge for a crisp finish.

Repeat with the pencil holder.

2. CREATE LOOPS IN PENCIL HOLDER

Place the pencil holder on top of pocket (right-side up). Line up the left edge and stitch through all layers to secure.

Create a loop by placing a pencil or your finger under the panel to space, then pin it to secure. Continue across the pencil panel to make as many pencil spots (or mini-pockets) as you'd like. Six pencil spots is probably good—who needs more than six pens and pencils? Think about making a fat spot for a chubby highlighter, too. Adjust the loops until the end of the pencil holder is even with the edge of the larger pocket.

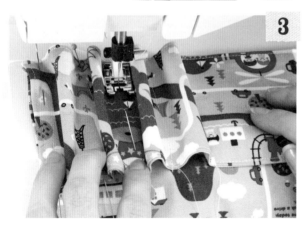

3. STITCH BETWEEN LOOPS

With the pencil loops pinned in place, take the pockets to your machine. Stitch the loops down securely by sewing between each loop from top to bottom (or bottom to top) and backstitching at each end.

Front and Back Panels

When the backpack is closed, the front and back panels are indeed the front and back. But when the backpack is laying flat, they'll be at the sides, like the pages in a book. Also, see page 24 for the Piping Crash Course as well as additional photos and instructions on applying piping.

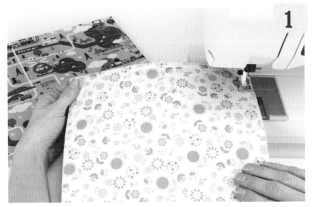

1. BASTE FRONT AND LINING

Place the front panel and lining panel wrong sides together and baste together around all four sides.

2. STITCH PENCIL HOLDER TO POCKET

On the wrong side of the front panel, the one with the lining fabric facing out, place the pocket and pencil holder so that the lower edges are ¾" (1.9cm) above the bottom raw edge of the front panel. Stitch along the two sides, from top to bottom, and backstitch at each end. Then, stitch along the lower edge of the pocket, taking care not to sew over the lower edge of the loops you made for the pencils—this will allow longer pencils to slide through and rest against the bottom of the backpack.

3. STITCH PIPING ON FRONT PANEL

On the right side of front panel (the panel without the pocket/pencil holder), apply piping. To do so, pin the length of the piping to all four edges. Start in the center of one edge (not at a corner) and leave the first few inches of piping unattached. As you come to each corner, stop ½" (1.3cm) from the end and snip into the seam allowance of the piping only—not the front panel—up to the stitches but not through them.

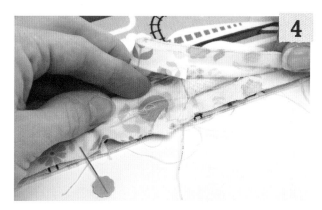

4. FINISH ADDING THE PIPING

When you get back to where you started pinning, you want to mask the ends of the piping. Trim the first end clean and then lay the two ends side by side and trim just the cording—not the bias tape—on the second end, so the two pieces of cording butt up against one another.

Fold under the raw edge of the second end of the bias tape and lay the first end inside it, right up against the second end. Wrap the bias tape back around and pin it in place.

5. BASTE PIPING IN PLACE

Using your zipper or piping foot, baste around the entire perimeter of the piping with your longest straight stitch. Set this panel aside for now, and we'll turn our attention to the bottom panel.

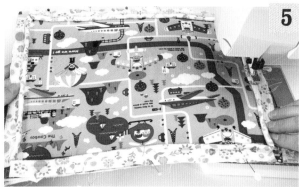

Bottom Panel

This is the base of the backpack and will have the lower straps sandwiched in the seam. With those seams sewn, you'll have basically a large circle that will form the outer edge of the backpack.

MATCH ZIPPER PANEL TO BOTTOM

Match the zipper panel on one end to one short side of the bottom panel. Zipper pulls should be at the center of the zipper and out of the way. Stitch ⅝" (1.6cm) seam, and press the seam allowances open. Repeat on the opposite end.

Straps

It's easiest to make the straps as two pieces, then clip off a chunk to make the lower strap, rather than making four separate straps of varying lengths.

1. FOLD AND PRESS STRAPS

Press the straps in half lengthwise down the center, then open the back out. Using the crease in the center as a guide, fold and press each long side in toward the crease, so you have a piece that has two folded edges that meet in the middle.

2. PRESS AGAIN

Press again along the original center crease to make a folded piece that has four thicknesses.

3. TOPSTITCH STRAP; CUT END

Topstitch along each long edge of the strap, then again on the folded side of the strap. Repeat with the opposite strap.

Cut the lower 6" (15.2cm) off each strap to make the lower strap.

4. ADD D-RING AND PIN STRAP TO BACKPACK

Place the D-ring on the lower strap, then fold in half. Repeat with the opposite lower strap. Then place the lower strap between the two small dots on the lower edge of the back panel (on the out/main fabric side). Keeping the lower straps folded with the D-ring attached, line up all the raw edges and pin securely in place.

Then place each upper strap between the two large dots on the same side panel—the upper strap should roughly line up with the lower strap, as they'll connect with one another to make the backpack wearable. Baste or pin securely in place.

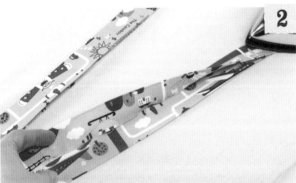

STITCH TIP

For super security, you might want to strongly consider basting the straps in place, just to prevent any weird rotational accidents that might cause the strap to shift as you sew.

Assemble the Body of the Backpack

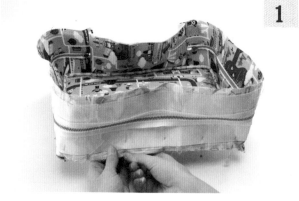

1

1. PIN ZIPPER PANEL TO FRONT PANEL

Place the circle zipper section right sides together and raw edges even with the piped front panel, centering the bottom panel seams on either side of the base of the front panel.

2. STITCH

Using a zipper or piping foot, stitch around all four sides to secure. Keep those stitches as snug up against the piping as you can, even going so far as to lightly pinch the fabric between your fingers before it goes under the needle.

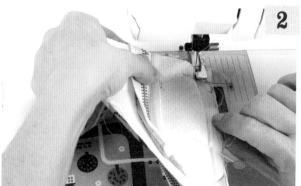

2

3. PIN AND STITCH ON BACK PANEL

Open the zipper slightly to allow room to reach in and turn right-side out later.

Take the back panel and place it right sides together with the zipper panel, just like you did with the front panel. Stitch all the way around using a ½" (1.3cm) seam allowance. Tuck the straps so they are out of the way as you stitch.

Using the opening in the zipper, unzip the rest of the way so that the backpack is now laying flat in front of you.

3

Bind the Edges

On the front/back panels, you'll notice that the inner seams are exposed with raw edges with the lining caught in them. We'll be wrapping them in bias tape to make the interior of the bag nice and clean. Begin by making some continuous bias tape, either from your lining fabric or from a contrasting fabric—I recommend a lighter, quilt-weight cotton, as the home dec fabrics are usually too thick for this step. You can also use your lining for the bias binding—it makes a really clean, continuous look on the interior if you do, just sayin'. (Also, see page 74 for more on double-fold bias tape.)

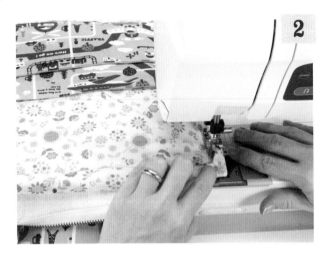

1. MAKE DOUBLE-FOLD BIAS TAPE

Cut bias tape to 1½" (3.8cm) wide. Using a 25mm (0.98") bias tape maker, press in the sides to the center. Press bias tape in half again, so you have four thicknesses with all the raw edges disguised.

2. STITCH BIAS TAPE OVER SEAMS

Beginning on the bottom panel, sandwich the seam allowances inside the bias tape like you're capturing the seams in a clamshell. Pin in place.

Stitch around all sides through the bias tape on both sides and the seam allowances in the center. At each corner, fold the binding around to the new edge, creating a mitered corner as you do—this is better imagined less as turning a corner than as wrapping a gift, where you let the excess make little triangle points as you take that 90-degree corner, then fold those triangle points flat on the new side. When you come around to where the bias tape overlaps, fold one end under and create a clean overlap where the join will be.

Reach through the opened zipper and turn the whole bag right-side out.

STITCH TIP

There are a lot of thicknesses here, so take your time. If you have trouble, try switching to a new needle or using a slightly larger needle size to help you get through all that fabric and interfacing.

NEXT STEPS

Zippers? You're the master now! Try another zipper by moving on to the **Sassy Pants** project (see page 196), this time with a fly!

Plenty of piping in this project—for a next step and some more piping, why not check out the **Footstool Slipcover** (see page 22) and make it sassy?

The straps on this make me think of the closure on the **A-Line Skirt** (see page 180)—move the skills you've used here over there, and master the art of the buckle.

LEVEL 5 | BOY'S LINED PEA COAT

What little boy doesn't make your heart melt when he's dressed in a classic pea coat? Use melton wool or heavy corduroy for this, and you'll have a heavy jacket for late fall. Melton wool is slightly felted, giving it heft and thickness to keep out winter winds; it makes an excellent choice if you haven't worked with wools before, as it is stable and behaves nicely under the needle. Corduroy's thickness is directly related to the wale, or width of the cords; a 21-wale means there are 21 cords per inch (2.5cm), and an 8-wale has 8 cords per inch (2.5cm). More cords means lighter-weight fabric, as the space between cords has fewer fibers to hold in warmth. Lining a jacket like this with a quilt-weight cotton gives you plenty of chances to give the jacket a pop of personality.

SUPPLIES

2 yds (1.8 m) of melton wool, wool tweed or heavy corduroy

2 yds (1.8 m) of cotton or lining fabric for lining

Fusible interfacing

Six 1" (2.5cm) buttons

Matching thread

Cut Fabric Pieces and Interface

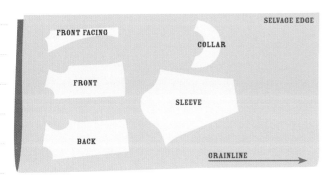

1. CUT JACKET PIECES

Begin by cutting all the pattern pieces: jacket fronts (2), jacket back (1, on fold), sleeve fronts and sleeve backs (2 of each), front facings (2), upper collar (1) and under collar (1). Pieces to cut from lining: jacket fronts (2), jacket back (1, on fold), sleeve fronts and sleeve backs (2 of each).

Pay attention to the notches and dots. Transfer all those markings to the wrong side of your fabric, since those will allow you to exactly match the bits as you assemble them together.

2. INTERFACE

Apply fusible interfacing to the jacket's right and left facings. Repeat with the under collar.

Coat Back

1. STITCH CENTER BACK SEAM

Stitch the center back seam with a ⅝" (1.6cm) seam allowance.

2. STAYSTITCH NECKLINE

Staystitch the neckline edge between notches. (Staystitching is designed to stabilize an edge that isn't on grain, to prevent it from stretching later. It's easy and only takes a second—so try to avoid the temptation to skip it. You'll thank me later.)

3. TOPSTITCH

Topstitch from the right side, ¼" (6.4mm) from the seamline, making a mock flat fell seam.

4. PRESS SEAM ALLOWANCES

Press the seam allowances to one side.

FLAT FELL SEAMS

This is the kind of detailing that really sets your handmade clothing apart. The flat fell seam is strong and reliable, and very easy to stitch. You'll see it on jeans and jackets, and in this case, it will really set your sewing off. For a true flat fell seam, begin with fabric right sides together and stitch a ¼" (6.4mm) seam allowance. Turn fabric wrong sides together and press, then stitch another seam on the wrong side that's ⅜" (19.5 mm). You'll have taken out ⅝" (1.6cm) total, but have a little flappy seam sticking up from your fabric. Fold that flap over to the side, press it down, then stitch again very close to the loose edge. That's a flat fell seam!

Jacket Front and Shoulders

1. STITCH FRONT/BACK TO SHOULDERS

Stitch the jacket front pieces to the jacket back at the shoulder seams using a ⅝" (1.6cm) seam allowance. Press the seam allowances toward the back.

2. TOPSTITCH RIGHT SIDES

Topstitch from the right sides, ¼" (6.4mm) from the seamline, to create another mock flat fell seam.

For now we'll leave the side seams open and unstitched to make putting in little sleeves a bit easier.

Under Collar

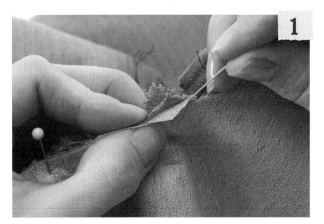

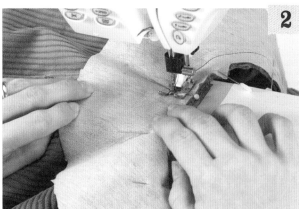

1. INTERFACE COLLAR
Apply interfacing to wrong side of one collar piece. Pin it carefully along the neckline edge, taking the time to match notches as you do.

2. STITCH COLLAR TO NECKLINE
Using a ⅝" (1.6cm) seam allowance, stitch the collar to the jacket neckline edge.

TRY THIS, TOO: LEATHER VERSION
Leather jackets make me think of Top Gun and men with big muscles. Working with leather doesn't require advanced military training or hours on the volleyball court to get you into shape. Most machines have plenty of muscle to handle sewing leather, so choose the right needle and jump right in. As you choose leather to work with, keep in mind that the number of ounces will directly affect how thick it is and how well your sewing machine's motor will handle the extra work. I recommend no more than three-ounce leather for this project—it's softer and more supple than heavier skins and will be easier to sew. Purchase your leather not by the yard but by the skin—most are around twelve to twenty square feet on average, which should be plenty for this project. Use a leather sewing machine needle for the sewing, and an all-polyester thread. Finally, rather than pressing seams open or to the side with your iron, pound them flat. That's right: Using a mallet or tailor's block, pound the skins to make the seams flatter and more malleable. It's super therapeutic, and the results look great.

Two-Part Sleeves

Most sleeves, called inset sleeves, are made by making the sleeve into a tube and then working to insert it into the armhole opening. Rather than doing that, we'll simplify the sleeve installation a bit and put it in flat. Now, this is a two-piece sleeve, so installing flat is a bit unusual, but because children's clothing is smaller than adult's, this method will make for a little bit easier work. If you would rather use a more classic tailoring approach to this jacket, by all means do so: Just sew the underarm seam and then insert the sleeve as in the Wherever Jacket on page 206.

1. STITCH SLEEVE FRONT AND BACK

Stitch the sleeve front to the sleeve back, matching notches and using a ⅝" (1.6cm) seam allowance. Press the seam allowances toward the back.

2. TOPSTITCH RIGHT SIDE

Topstitch from the right side, ¼" (6.4mm) from the seamline (another mock flat fell seam).

Stitch the same seam for the sleeve lining, pressing the seam allowances open.

3. EASESTITCH UPPER EDGE

Easestitch along the curved upper edge of the sleeve, using a ½" (1.3cm) seam allowance. Remember, ease stitches are used to adjust the amount of fullness along a seam line—kind of like a gather, but not nearly so dramatic. Use your longest straight stitch, once at the seam line and again ¼" (6.4mm) inside the seam allowance. Leave nice, long thread tails to adjust the ease in a bit when we insert the sleeve to the sleeve opening.

4. CHECK FOR CORRECT SLEEVE; MATCH NOTCHES

For the flat installation approach, note that you'll be placing a convex curve into a concave one. Notches are here to make this process simpler by marking what section of each curve matches the opposite side. Double notches indicate the back of the garment, so be sure you're working with the correct sleeve!

5. PLACE SLEEVE TOGETHER WITH ARMHOLE CURVE

Place the sleeve right sides together with the armhole curve. Match the top of the sleeve with the shoulder seam. Place a pin at this center point, then pin at each notch. It's okay here if there is some extra volume between the notches—you'll ease that out in the next step.

6. PIN SLEEVE TO ARMHOLE

Work your way around the sleeve cap, pinning and adjusting as you go. Adjust the ease at the top of the sleeve cap—the curviest part, where the sleeve will fit into the armhole—by manipulating the threads of your ease stitching until the tube fits just right inside the armhole. You should get a nice, clean fit with no lumps or bumps, just slight easing gathers.

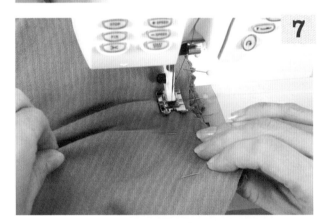

7. STITCH

Stitch a ⅝" (1.6cm) seam allowance, taking care to prevent any puckering or pleating as you sew. You'll notice as the eased seamline goes beneath the needle, that the excess volume shifts to one side or the other of the stitches—this is what easing is meant to do. Just take care that you don't get any accidental pleating. When you've come back to the beginning, backstitch and then press the seam allowances toward the sleeve.

8. STITCH ARM SEAM

With the sleeve successfully installed, adjust the jacket sleeve and front so that the underarm seam comes together—you'll have the sleeve make a tube, and the jacket front and jacket back right sides together at the side seam. Stitch this seam from wrist to hem, across the ends of the armhole seam, all in one go.

Lining and Collar

Many of these steps mirror those of the outer jacket, so a lot of this sewing is review. It gets more exciting in a minute, so be brave, little toaster.

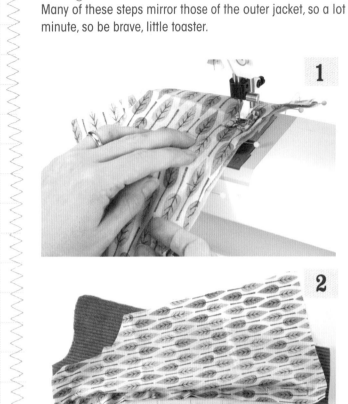

1. STITCH LINING CENTER BACK SEAM

Stitch the center back seam of the back lining. Press it open.

2. STITCH FRONT FACING TO LINING; FRONT TO BACK LINING

Stitch the front facing to the lining. Stitch the front lining to the back lining at the shoulders.

3. STITCH UPPER COLLAR TO NECKLINE

Place the upper collar together with neckline edge of the front facing and lining. Stitch as you did the under collar.

4. STITCH LINING ARM SEAMS

Stitch the underarm seam of sleeve lining. Stitch the armhole seam for the lining as you did for the outer jacket.

Place the lining and outer jacket right sides together, slipping the sleeves into the sleeve linings as you do.

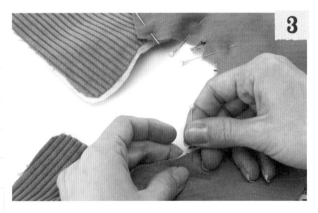

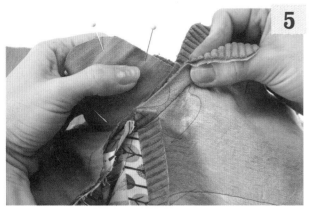

5. PUT UNDER COLLAR AND UPPER COLLAR TOGETHER

Keep the seam allowances pulled away from the seam and toward the collar so they aren't caught in the seam here. This will prevent any weird puckering and create a smooth collar that will lie flat. Take care as you put the upper collar and under collar right sides together that you face all your seam allowances toward the collar. They won't stay open here—having them toward the collar will help it to lie flat later. Repeat on the opposite side.

6. PIN

Match all notches and circles and pin everything in place.

7. STITCH LOWER FRONT EDGE

Begin stitching at the lower front edge of one jacket front, all the way up to the dot on the collar. Stop and backstitch, taking care not to catch the seam allowances—they should remain free so you can manipulate them a bit.

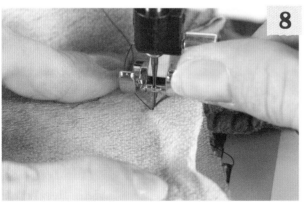

8. COMPLETE COLLAR SEAM

Fold the seam allowances the other way and complete the collar seam, picking up the seamline and stitching around the collar to the small dot at the opposite seamline. Take care to backstitch at the beginning and end of each seam. Trim the seam allowances.

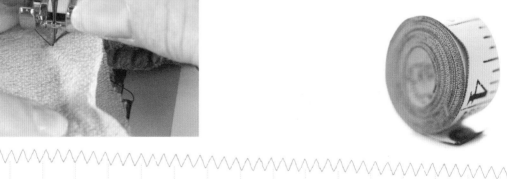

9. PUT SLEEVE LINING INSIDE SLEEVES; TOPSTITCH

Turn right-side out. With the entire upper and front edge of the jacket stitched, lay the jacket so that it's completely inside out—that is, put the sleeve linings inside the sleeves and have the rest of the jacket lining flat up against the outer fabric, but inside out. When you've done this, you ought to see the collar seam allowances sticking out a bit. Grab hold of those and press them together, then stitch through all thicknesses, about ¼" (6.4mm) from the raw edges. This will prevent them from moving around inside the collar and creating odd bulky bits. Press and steam all seams nice and smooth. Topstitch from lower edge to lower edge, across the collar.

10. CLIP SEAM ALLOWANCES

Clip into the seam allowances at each of the curved sections, including making a deep snip at the juncture where the collar meets the jacket front, right up to the stitches, but not through them.

11. TRIM SEAM ALLOWANCES

In some places, like at the points of the collar, trimming the seam allowances will make for a smoother finish and easier turning. Trim down to ¼" (6.4mm) seam allowance.

12. TURN RIGHT-SIDE OUT

Turn the whole puppy right-side out, using a chopstick or bamboo knitting needle to get into those itty bitty spots and encourage them gently to pop into pretty shapes.

Hem and Finish

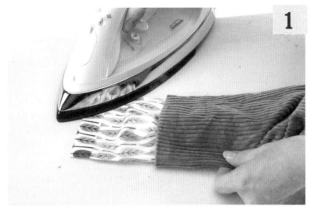

1. FOLD HEM OF SLEEVE
On the lower edge of the sleeve, pull the lining away from the sleeve and press under sleeve lining. Pull the lining out of the way and turn up the hem on the outer jacket and press in place. Make sure the lining is hemmed ¼" (6.4mm) shorter than outer jacket so it can't be seen.

2. TOPSTITCH SLEEVE
Allow the sleeve and lining to fall naturally, then topstitch the sleeve hem close to the edge of the garment.

3. FOLD JACKET HEM
Turn up the remainder of the jacket hem, pressing as you go. Turn under 1" (2.5cm) of lining. Press it in place.

4. TOPSTITCH JACKET HEM
Slipstitch the hem at the folded edge. Topstitch the lower hemline.

Buttons and Buttonholes

The classic pea coat look includes four or six buttons, double-breasted. You can use fewer, but the lapels flap down most attractively if you stick with four or six in a two-by-two configuration.

1. STITCH BUTTONHOLES

Using the markings on the pattern pieces, set the buttonholes and stitch them in place. Clip open the holes. (Check out the Crash Course on buttonholes on the next page, as needed.)

2. STITCH ON BUTTONS

Add buttons with a shank.

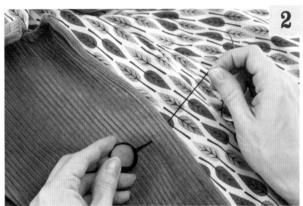

CRASH COURSE: BUTTONHOLES

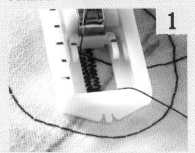 **1**

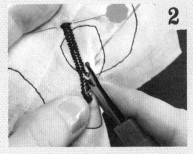 **2**

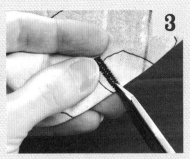 **3**

Mark button length and line up your buttonhole foot on the chalk line. Using your buttonhole function, stitch down one side and then make a bar tack at the end. Stitch the second side of the buttonhole, and then complete the other bar tack.

Use your seam ripper to open up the fabric in between the two rows of stitches, OR...

Use a small pair of scissors by folding the buttonhole in half and snipping the opening.

Not all coats are the same. Here, you mastered a lined coat with a lay-flat sleeve. Move on to the **Wherever Jacket** (see page 206) and conquer the unlined coat with the set-in sleeve! It's the same, but different!

Corduroy makes such a fantastic choice for this coat. I like to use corduroy as an unexpected fabric in handbags, too, which leads me to suggest the **Classy Lady Elbow Bag** (see page 118) as the perfect next step for you. Plus: buttons!

Like a lining now and then? Turn to the **Reversible Girl's Dress** (see page 132) and see how a lining can really be a whole new look.

NEXT STEPS

SECTION 5:
CLOTHING

When I first learned to sew, I only ever thought of sewing clothing. It was what my mother made, and her mother before her. It seemed practical and familiar and I wanted to make clothes more than anything in the world. I still love sewing apparel, and feel a very specific type of satisfaction when I try on a garment I have made myself and find that it fits right and feels good, and know with total certainty that no one else has something just like it. There are usually more steps to sewing a garment, but in the end, it's really all sewing a seam—not that different from any of the other projects in this book. If you've been sewing straight lines for a while, but are putting off making clothes, these patterns will take you into a whole new territory that is as addictive as it is exhilarating. I'm a big believer in simple wardrobe staples, the kind with classic lines that let the fabric be the star. Feel free to indulge yourself a little here and buy some really special fabric for your garments—you'll never feel as pretty as you do walking down the street in a fabulous piece of clothing you made yourself. Viva la sewing!

LEVEL 1 | KNIT TOP

Very few things in my wardrobe get the kind of nonstop wear that my knit tops do. I'm a bit too grown-up to wear a T-shirt every day, but I'm still far too lazy to iron anytime I need to leave the house and look like a human. Enter the adult knit top. Just enough styling to make it look polished, not so much that you seem like you're trying too hard. You will wear this top every single day until they have to pry it from your fingers. I recommend a jersey knit for this project, and you'll be pleased to know that it sews up fast and lovely on just your sewing machine—no fancy special tools or equipment required.

SUPPLIES

1½ yds (1.37 m) of jersey knit (cotton, rayon, or wool)

Matching thread

Ballpoint machine needle

¼ yd (0.23 m) of knit tricot interfacing

Cut Fabric Pieces

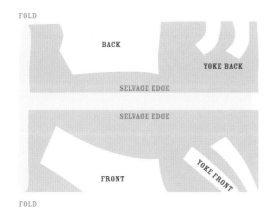

CUT

Begin by cutting all the pattern pieces: one front, cut on fold; one back, cut on fold; two sleeves (one right and one left); two neck pieces, cut on fold.

Note that all pieces are cut on the fold with the exception of the sleeves. Remember to cut sleeves mirrored to one another so you'll have one right and one left.

TIPS FOR PREPPING AND CUTTING KNITS

• Be careful when laying out your fabric to cut to keep it all ON the cutting surface—fabric left hanging off the end of the table can weight down and stretch the rest of the fabric, distorting your pieces.

• If you have to stretch or spread your fabric when laying it out to cut, let it sit for fifteen minutes or so to "bounce" back into shape before cutting.

• Use pattern weights rather than pins and a small rotary cutter rather than shears for really accurate cutting.

• Try taping the edges of your knits to the cutting surface if they're especially slippery—this can anchor them without needing pins or weights, and allows you to get really accurate cuts.

• There is no need to press knit fabrics prior to working with them, but do be careful to prewash! Knits shrink a great deal more than wovens, and while they do stretch, don't make them have to stretch too much because they got smaller in the dryer, okay?

• I recommend using your rotary cutter—I particularly like my 28mm rotary cutter.

Just like knitting with yarn on needles, knit fabrics have a knit side and a purl side--what we'd call a right side and a wrong side on woven fabrics. The knit side will be slightly smoother and may show the Vs. of the knit stitch.

Side Seams

Knit fabrics can be a bit tricky to work with if you're accustomed to only sewing wovens. Jersey and other knits can roll at the edges in way that woven fabrics don't, which can take some getting used to. Just take your time and you'll be fine. Be sure to swap out your sewing machine needle for a ballpoint machine needle and take your time pinning!

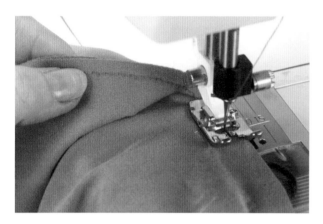

STITCH SIDE SEAMS

Place shirt front and shirt back right sides together, matching the side seams. Stitch. When you're finished, you'll notice a weirdly shaped void at the neckline—this is where the sleeves fit, so don't fret!

Sleeves

Many patterns ask you to create what are known as "inset" sleeves, where a sleeve tube is fitted into the shirt opening. (If you complete the Wherever Jacket at the end of this chapter, then you'll become familiar with this process.) For thicker fabrics, this is an excellent way to get a really great fit, but with lighter fabrics and especially knits, the inset method is a little finicky and unnecessarily complicated. Instead, we're making raglan sleeves that form both the sleeve and the shoulder of the shirt and have the added advantage of being super easy to install.

See how the opening for the sleeves are asymmetrical? Also notice that the back is higher than the front—paying attention to this will help you get the correct sleeve on the correct side.

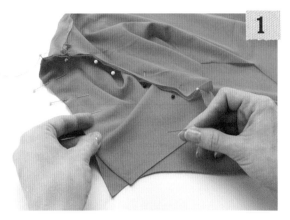

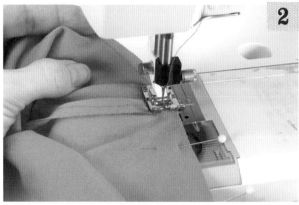

1. STITCH UNDERARM SEAMS; PIN SLEEVE TO SHIRT

Sew up the underarm seam using a ¼" (6.4mm) seam allowance. Turn right-side out.

Place the sleeve right sides together with the inside-out shirt, matching notches and lining the side seam up with the underarm seam. Pin.

2. STITCH SLEEVE TO SHIRT

Stitch a ¼" (6.4mm) seam allowance around the entire sleeve. Repeat with the opposite sleeve.

Set the whole thing aside while you make the yoke and bring this bad boy home.

Gather the Neckline

1. TRANSFER DOTS; INSTALL GATHERING STITCHES

Transfer the dots from the pattern indicating where to begin and end the gathering stitches. Place a pin at each dot, then, using a long, straight stitch, install gathering stitches from pin to pin.

2. PULL TO CREATE GATHERS

Pull up on them a little more than you think you'll need to—we'll attach the yoke here, and the gathers will fall oh-so-gracefully below it.

Complete the Neckline

For the yoke (neckline), you'll be adding tricot interfacing. Tricot interfacing works the same way as interfacings for woven fabrics, but has a little give to it. Using an interfacing here isn't essential and can be eliminated if you've struggled to find some (see the resources in the back for online shops that carry it). But you'll find that using it helps the neckline lie flatter and prevents sagging and gaping, and makes a major difference in how smooth your seams are and how pretty your topstitching turns out.

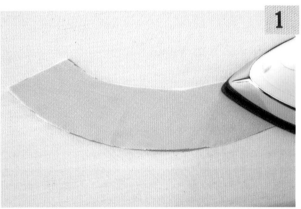

1. INTERFACE ONE YOKE FRONT AND BACK
Apply fusible knit tricot interfacing to one yoke front and one yoke back piece (remaining pieces will be used for facings).

2. STITCH YOKE FRONT AND BACK TOGETHER
Stitch the interfaced yoke front and yoke back together at the shoulder seams. Repeat with uninterfaced pieces (which are the yoke facings).

3. STITCH YOKE AND YOKE FACING TOGETHER
Place the yoke facing right sides together with yoke at the upper edge. Stitch a ¼" (6.4mm) seam, taking care to pivot at the point.

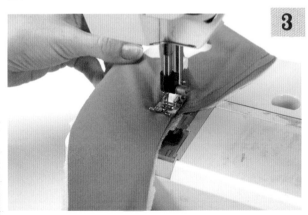

CUTTING INTERFACING TO SIZE—OR NOT?
I always prefer to fuse a piece of interfacing that is slightly larger than the fabric and then trim the excess after they're fused together. But you can absolutely cut a piece of interfacing using the pattern piece so that the two are the exact same size before fusing—technically, the latter is the more correct method, but I stand by my cheating.

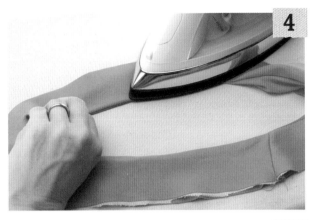

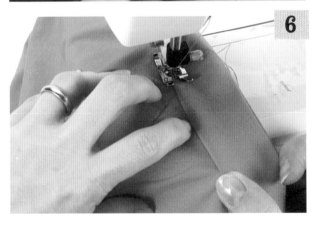

YOKE AND FACINGS EXPLAINED

A yoke is in many ways a glorified collar, but is usually wider than a collar would be, and crosses between the shoulders of a shirt. In our case, the yoke goes around the neckline, is wider than a collar would be and forms the upper edge of the sleeves.

A facing is an interior garment piece that serves to back a portion of the garment and, when sewn, to create a finished edge. Facings can appear at waistlines, hemlines and collars. Here, the facing is a duplicate of the yoke and lets us finish off the upper edge of the shirt.

4. STEAM AND TOPSTITCH YOKE

Using a hint of steam at the iron, turn the yoke facing to the inside, steaming to get a good, smooth finish.

Topstitch the upper edge of the yoke all the way around, again pivoting at the point. Baste the lower edge of the neckline and facing to stabilize it before attaching it to the body of the shirt.

5. STITCH YOKE-GATHERED EDGE

Matching notches and shoulder seams, place the yoke right sides together with the gathered neckline edge of shirt, holding the unfinished lower edges of the yoke and facing together. Stitch a ¼" (6.4mm) seam.

6. PRESS AND TOPSTITCH

Press the seam allowances toward the yoke and topstitch close to the seamline.

Trim away any excess interfacing on the inside of the garment using super sharp scissors—I like my appliqué scissors for this job because the large leaf-shaped blade really pulls the fabric away from the shirt and prevents me from accidentally snipping into the fabric.

Topstitch With a Double Needle

A double needle is like a single needle, but there are two of them. Clever, right? Really all a double needle does is allow you to send two strands of thread through the machine at the same time. Add your second spool holder (if you have a removable one) or bust out a crème brulee dish and lay your spare spool there. Handy tip: Have your two spools rotating in opposite directions to avoid tangling the threads as you sew.

1. FOLD HEM AND PIN

Turn up the hem on your sleeves and lower edge of the shirt. (The pattern allows for ½" [1.3cm], but you make them the length you need them to be.) Hold or pin these in place and then go sew them. Take care not to stretch the fabric as you sew, or you'll end up with puckers—it might look like I'm pulling on the fabric in the image, but you totally don't want to put any tension on it as it moves beneath your needle.

2. TOPSTITCH HEM

Using the double needle and two spools of thread, topstitch the hemlines, getting a nice professional-looking finish.

TRY THIS, TOO: BEADED VARIATION

With very little work, you can transform this basic pattern into a dozen different shirts that look very little like one another. Adding simple beading on the yoke can dress this up for an evening out with your honey or just so you look extra pretty in the carpool line.

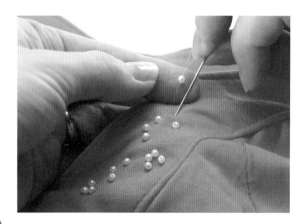

To make the beading stitches as invisible as possible, add the beads to the interfaced yoke before stitching it to the yoke facing. Use a nylon filament thread—which looks like clear plastic thread, but is very strong and slightly stretchy—so that your attention will be on the beads and not the stitches. Add as many or as few beads as you like, keeping in mind that the fabric will have to hold the weight of them. Lighter seed beads are best, and small glass beads can lend an air of luxury.

Working with new and unfamiliar fabrics can be an exciting challenge. Check out the **Boy's Lined Pea Coat** (see page 158) with its leather variation and see how exciting a new fiber can really be!

This top uses simple gathers to create shape at the base of a V-neckline. Take that same idea and make the **Footstool Slipcover** with its gathered skirt (see page 22)— such a simple way to manipulate fabric and make it really come alive.

Pair this top with the **Sassy Pants** (see page 196) and make an outfit that you'll want to wear everywhere you go!

NEXT STEPS

LEVEL 2 | A-LINE SKIRT WITH PEEKABOO PLEAT

Fine, I admit it: I love me a sexy librarian look. It's true. As a card-carrying nerdophile, there is something about a classic, buttoned-down look that makes me feel both pretty and prim at the same time. This clean skirt, with its a-line shape and peekaboo pleat, has it all wrapped up. Making the pleat is simple, adding the pocket gives a touch of color and the delicious D-ring belted closure means neither zippers NOR buttons for you. It's like a skirt paradise. Make this one up in heavier fabrics, like twill, corduroy, wools or denim. The inset for the pleat can be any fabric you choose—may I suggest something truly special that you've been saving for just such an occasion?

SUPPLIES

1½ yds (1.37 m) of bottomweight cotton, linen, denim or wool for the skirt body

½ yd (0.46 m) of contrast fabric for the pleat and pocket

Matching thread

¼ yd (0.23 m) of mid-weight interfacing

1 D-ring or buckle

Cut Fabric Pieces

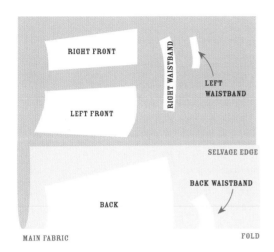

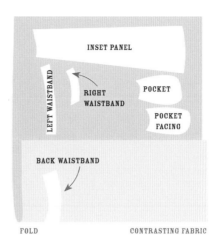

1. CUT

Begin by cutting all the pattern pieces: From your main skirt fabric, cut one skirt right, one skirt left front and one skirt back. From your contrast fabric, cut the pocket, pocket lining and the inset panel. From the waistband pieces, cut one each of the main fabric and the contrast.

2. ADD INTERFACING

Add interfacing to the back waistband, right waistband and left waistband pieces.

Skirt Back and Front, Including Pleat Panel

We will be creating a box pleat for this simple skirt. With a box pleat, the goal is to make the pleat peekaboo from inside the skirt when you walk, like a delicious surprise that only you know about—for now.

1. STITCH DARTS IN SKIRT BACK

Stitch the two darts in the skirt back. Press toward the center. (Turn to the next page for the Crash Course on stitching darts, if you need it.)

CRASH COURSE: STITCHING DARTS

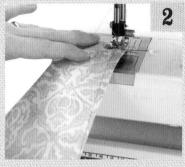

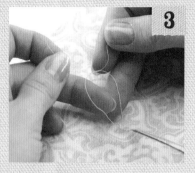

1. Using the marks on your pattern, transfer all darts and dots to the wrong side of your fabrics. I like to use an air-soluble pen for this, but if you don't think you'll be marking and sewing on the same day, use a water-soluble pen.

2. Always begin sewing a dart at the larger end, heading toward the point. Don't stop and backstitch at the point! Instead, reduce your stitch length as you approach it, then sew very close to the edge of the fold as you sew off the point.

3. At the point of each dart, use the extra thread tails you've left to tie a knot by hand. Never backtack to secure a dart—it adds bulk and an odd pointiness. Instead, always tie a hand knot, then trim the excess threads.

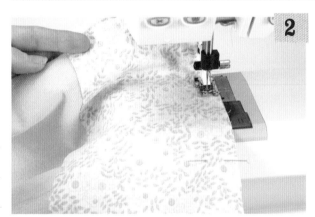

2. SEW SIDE FRONT AND PLEAT PANEL TOGETHER

Place the side front right sides together with the pleat panel and stitch a notched edge using a ¼" (6.4mm) seam allowance.

3. STITCH LEFT FRONT AND PLEAT PANEL TOGETHER

Place the left front panel right sides together with the opposite long edge of the pleat panel and repeat.

Press the seam allowances toward the pleat panel.

STITCH TIP

On all of these interior seams, if you plan to finish the seam—overlock or pink your seams to keep them tidy on the inside after you launder your skirt—do so as soon as that particular seam is sewn. I like to overcast all the edges of my pieces before I begin sewing by stitching a zigzag over the raw edge around all sides

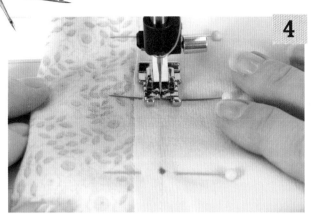

4. STITCH PLEAT PANEL SEAMS

From the right side, bring the pleat panel seams together, right sides facing. Stitch a vertical seam from the upper edge to the small dot. Backstitch at end of seam.

5. PRESS PLEAT

Press the pleat flat by centering the panel over the seam you just stitched and making the "box" of the pleat.

Flip the skirt so the front is facing up and press down the pleat panel to make the edges of the seams nice and crisp, which will keep the pleat hidden (unless you're wearing the skirt, of course).

Make the Pocket

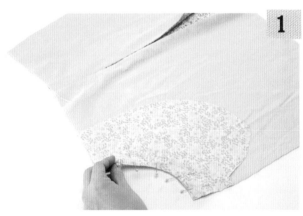

1. STITCH POCKET FACING

Place the pocket facing on the side front at the notched curve, with right sides together. Pin in place.

Stitch using a ⅝" (1.6cm) seam allowance, taking care to keep the seam nice and smoothly curved.

2. PIN POCKET AND FACING TOGETHER

Press the seam allowances toward the pocket facing. Place the pocket facing right sides together with the pocket—remember, the pocket facing will be toward you as you wear the skirt, and the pocket will be visible to the public. Pin in place. Then stitch the curved edge around the outside of these two pieces using a ⅝" (1.6cm) seam allowance.

3. TURN TOWARD SKIRT FRONT

Turn the whole thing toward the skirt front—nothing here has to be turned inside out, just flipped as a set so that the pocket will lie flat against the interior of the skirt front and the upper edge of the pocket will form a new side edge.

Stitch the Side Seams

STITCH SKIRT SIDE SEAMS

Place the skirt front and skirt back right sides together and pin in place. Stitch the seams using a ⅝" (1.6cm) seam allowance. (Did you notice that now, the side seam of the skirt front includes the pocket edge, too? Isn't that cool? Just wait until we get to the part where this skirt has no zipper OR buttons.) Press seam allowances open on both side seams once you're done gloating over what a great job you're doing.

Add the Waistband

1. STITCH WAISTBAND PIECES TOGETHER

Place left and right waistband pieces right sides together with the back waistband (at opposite ends) and pin. Stitch ⅝" (1.6cm) seams. Press seam allowances open. You now have one long waistband piece.

2. CREATE BIAS TAPE AND STITCH TO POCKET

To finish off the upper edge of the pocket and pocket facing, let's call on our old, trusted friend bias tape, shall we? Cut a short piece of fabric on the bias, which is to say, diagonal to the grain line. You don't need much—about 8" × 2" (20.3cm × 5.1cm). Fold in one long edge ½" (1.3cm) and press. Pin the other long edge to the upper edge of the pocket and pocket facing, across the seam, so that you've caught all the raw edge there. Stitch, using a ½" (1.3cm) seam allowance.

3. STITCH NEAR FOLDED EDGE

Press the bias tape to the wrong side, making it nice and smooth. The folded edge should cover your stitch line. Stitch very close to the folded edge to secure.

4. STITCH ON WAISTBAND

Place the waistband, all stitched into one piece, right sides together with the skirt. Match the side seams. Pin everything in place, then stitch using a ⅝" (1.6cm) seam allowance. You ought to begin and end at the pocket opening, not sewing on the pocket fabric itself—you won't be putting in a zipper on this skirt, so that pocket is your way in and out!

5. PLACE FACING ON WAISTBAND

Place the waistband facing right sides together with the waistband, matching dots and seams. Press under the bottom edge of the waistband facing ½" (1.3cm).

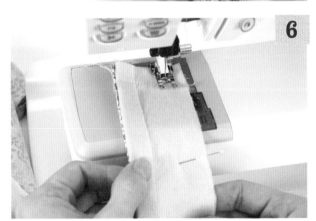

6. STITCH FACING IN PLACE

Beginning at the lower edge of the front waistband, stitch a ⅝" (1.6cm) seam around three sides of the waistband pieces, leaving the lower edge where the band extends beyond the skirt front unstitched.

7. FLIP AND PRESS

Flip the waistband facing to the inside and press firmly. Be sure to clip the point at the corner and use a turning tool to get a nice, clean edge!

8. TOPSTITCH WAISTBAND

Topstitch around the entire waistband, catching the lower edge and securing it as you do.

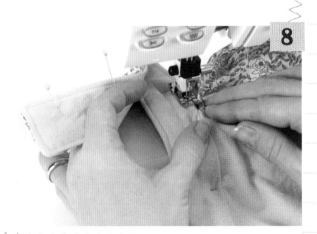

Install the Buckle

1. ADD D-RING TO WAISTBAND

At the waistband buckle end, slip two D-rings onto the waistband. Fold the end of the waistband over the straight portion of the buckles.

2. STITCH IN PLACE

Fold under and adjust the waistband end until you're satisfied with the amount of slack on the buckles. With the buckles out of the way, stitch securely in place, up and down to "knot" the stitches.

3. OPERATE THE BUCKLE

To operate the D-ring buckle, slip the buckle tab through the round portion of both rings, then reverse the end of the tab through one ring only. Tug to tighten. Since bodies are all different, you may find you want to shorten this tab. Feel free to snip off the end, then tuck the edges back inside to your desired length before re-sewing the topstitching.

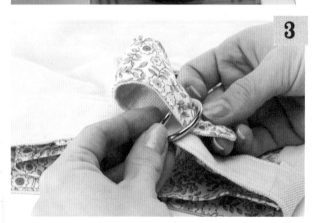

Hem the Skirt

1

At the lower edge, turn up ¼" (6.4mm) and press in place. Turn up another 1" (2.5cm) and press again. Stitch the hem at the inner fold.

TRY THIS, TOO: CROSS-STITCH, EMBROIDERY OR PATCHWORK BOX PLEAT PANEL

Consider dressing up this skirt even more by amping up the box pleat panel! Since it's a little "surprise" anyway, why not make it a big one? Choose to embroider the inset panel, or even make it entirely of patchwork to give it a super special zing. That way, when you walk or sit, you'll have something to look forward to, peeping out of the edge of your skirt. Fancy.

The hardware you use here is very similar to the hardware used for the strap on the **Everyday Shoulder Bag** (see page 100). Check out that project next to expand your skills using it!

Mixing and matching fabrics is a skill that improves over time, with practice and experimentation. The more you do it, the more confident you'll become. For your next step, move on to the **Tea Cozy and Friends** (see page 76) and mix up some new fabrics to see where those colors will lead you.

NEXT STEPS

LEVEL 3 | ENCHANTMENT UNDER THE SEA DRESS

Just the thing for feeding that retro-vibe void in your closet! Make it up in anything from cotton to chiffon, and you'll totally change the vibe—it's perfect for picnics by the lake, dressing up for the school dance, maybe even sitting in a parked car with a boy. Adding a store-bought crinoline underneath creates volume and vintage drama; leaving it out makes for a simple silhouette that flatters every figure. The fold-over detail at the bodice looks complicated but is simple to achieve, and can be stitched in a contrasting fabric for even more visual interest! Best part, at least for me? Leave off the straps and wear it as a super-flattering but still modest strapless number.

SUPPLIES

2½ to 3 yds (2.3 m-2.7 m) of dress-weight cotton or silk

½ yd (0.46 m) of coordinating fabric for the bodice lining

17" (43.2 cm) invisible zipper

Mid-weight fusible interfacing

Matching thread

Cut Fabric Pieces

CUT PIECES

Begin by cutting all the pattern pieces: bodice front (1, on fold), bodice back (2), skirt front (1, on fold), skirt back (2), pocket (4), bodice front lining (1 on fold), bodice back lining (2).

For the straps, cut a length of fabric 1½" (3.8cm) wide by 30" (76.2cm) long. This can be a cross-cut strip of fabric, cut from selvage to selvage.

SIZES 10-22

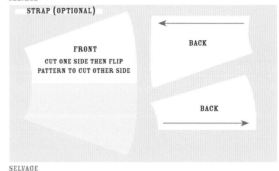

SIZES 2-8

Make Bodice

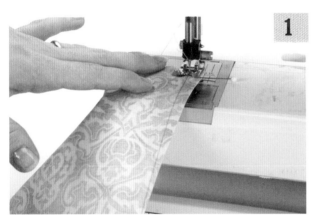

1. STITCH DARTS

Stitch darts at the waist on the bodice front and bodice back. These allow for graceful shaping, and are designed for a B or C cup. Remember, always begin sewing a dart at the larger end, heading toward the point. And never backtack; tie a hand knot. (See page 182 for a Crash Course on darts.)

Press toward the center. Repeat with the lining. (As with bags or other projects, anything you do to the outer shell of the dress, you'll need to do the same to the lining so the two will fit together.)

2. STITCH BODICE TOGETHER

Place the bodice front right sides together with bodice back. Stitch the side seams using a ⅝" (1.6cm) seam allowance. Press seam allowances open.

Repeat with the lining.

Pockets and Skirt

I mean, really: what's a pretty dress if it doesn't have pockets?

1 **1. STITCH POCKET TO SKIRT**

Place the pocket right sides together with the skirt front, matching the notches. Stitch a ⅝" (1.6cm) seam. Press seam allowances toward the pocket. Repeat with the opposite pocket. Repeat again with the skirt backs.

2. STITCH SKIRT FRONT AND BACK

Place the skirt front and skirt backs right sides together, matching pockets and notches. Pin in place. Stitch the side seams, sewing down to the dot, pivoting, sewing a ⅜" (9.5mm) seam around the body of the pockets up to the large dot, then pivoting at the hairpin curve and completing the seam.

3. CLIP INTO SEAM ALLOWANCE

Clip into the seam allowance above and below each pocket at the dot. Snip to the stitches but not through them, releasing the pockets from their bondage. Then press open the seams above and below the pocket.

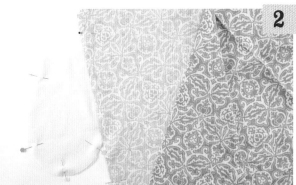

4. ATTACH SKIRT TO BODICE

Place the skirt right sides together with the bodice lower edge, matching notches and side seams. Stitch. With the side seams completed and the bodice all stitched up, place the bodice and skirt right sides together, matching those side seams. Stitch a ⅝" (1.6cm) seam from one side to the other.

Press seam allowances toward the bodice.

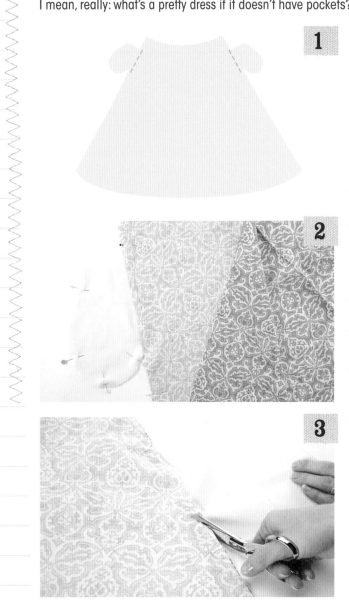

Install Invisible Zipper

I love a good invisible zipper, especially in a fitted dress. You can absolutely use a universal zipper here, or even one with nice metal teeth if you want a vintage vibe; the fit is the same with either! If you're unfamiliar with the ins and outs of how to install an invisible zipper, check out the Crash Course on the next page.

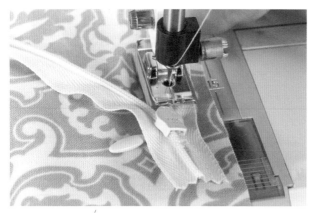

INSTALL ZIPPER

At the center back opening, insert the invisible zipper. The zigzag, upper edge of the zipper tape should be even with the upper edge of the bodice; the lower edge can fall anywhere, so long as it's below the waistline seam—a too-short zipper that ends before the waist, or even at it, will result in a dress you can't get into with any amount of trying.

Complete sewing the remainder of the center back seam from below the invisible zipper down to the hemline.

CRASH COURSE: INSTALLING AN INVISIBLE ZIPPER

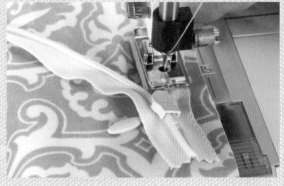

1. The secret to an invisible zipper is getting the teeth right on the seam line. If you're using an invisible zipper presser foot, which has a channel for guiding the teeth, this is much easier. First, press the teeth open using the iron. Then line them up with the seam line, and allow the teeth to fit into the groove of the invisible zipper foot.

2. Continue stitching along the zipper until the tip of the zipper foot touches the zipper pull and you can stitch no further. Backtack to secure.

3. To make the "invisible" part of the invisible zipper work, the teeth are pointed at the interior of the garment, and then will flip over and take the seam allowances with them. So for the second side of the zipper, you'll have to make a funny twist at the bottom—see that? When you see that the two sets of teeth are pointed away from one another, you'll know you're in good shape. Stitch the second side same as the first.

4. When both sides of the zipper are stitched in place, zip it up to make sure that everything is even and the waistline seam is still nice and straight. If so, finish the remainder of the side seam by starting a ⅝" (1.6cm) seam right NEXT to where the stitches end for the zipper legs. You'll want to pull the zipper out of the way and pinch it in half in order to squish it and keep your seam nice and flat. Backstitch, then sew all the way to the hemline. Press the entire length of the zipper from the right side of the garment.

Add the Straps

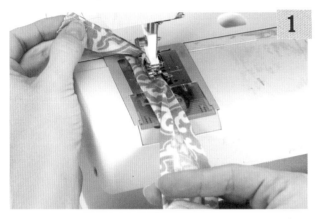

1. FOLD AND SEW STRAPS

Press the strap pieces in ¼" (6.4mm) on each long edge of the straps then press again in half. Stitch down both long edges to secure and topstitch simultaneously. Cut the strap in half to make two identical straps, each 15" (38.1cm) long.

2. PIN STRAP TO BODICE

Place one raw edge of the strap at the large dot on each bodice front. Pin in place, taking care to make sure the strap doesn't shift or rotate—you want them nice and straight. Consider using two or even three pins here, just to be safe.

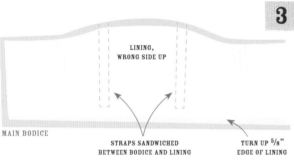

3. PRESS EDGE OF BODICE LINING

Press under the lower edge of the bodice lining ⅝" (1.6cm) — when you connect the bodice and the bodice lining later, you'll want to cover the seam with the lining to make the insides of your dress nice and pretty. Pressing them under is much easier now than it will be once the bodice is assembled, so it's really just advance planning.

Place the lining right sides together with the bodice, catching the strap between the two. Pin around the upper edge of the bodice, matching side seams and notches.

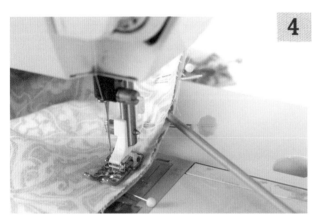

4. STITCH UPPER EDGE OF BODICE

Stitch around the upper edge of the bodice, catching the straps in the seam, taking care to leave an opening (indicated here with the wooden skewer) between each of the two sets of squares at the bodice back—these will allow the back end of the straps to remain free so you can adjust the strap length once the dress is on.

5. ADJUST AND FINISH STRAPS

Turn the bodice lining to the inside and press along the upper edge until everything is super duper crisp.

Reach between the bodice and lining to the opening you left on the side back—this is where the strap will peek through. Leaving this open allows you to try on the dress and adjust the length of the strap so it's just right for your torso. Pass the raw end of the strap through the opening and adjust (or have someone else help you adjust) until the bodice is just where you want it. Pin in place.

Either hand-stitch the straps in place (for an invisible finish) or topstitch around the entire upper edge of the bodice (for a more informal look).

So, we're going to do a little bit more hand-stitching to finish this thing off. I know, I know: you're thinking, "Deborah, you're not usually so into hand-stitching!" You're right, I'm not. But when I make a garment I really love, it's worth a few meditative minutes to get really pretty results, and nothing makes for quite so clean and chic a finish as does some hand-stitching. You caught me.

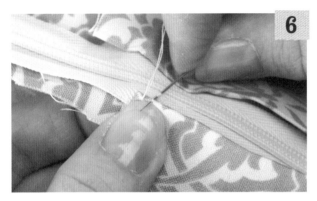

6. HAND-STITCH LINING

At the center back opening, place the pressed-under edge of the lining up against the inside zipper tape. Hand-stitch it in place.

7. SECURE THE LINING

At the waistline, lay the pressed-up lower edge of the lining over the seam allowances and pin in place. Hand-stitch on the inside or stitch the ditch from the public side of the dress to secure the lining—that would be the faster way and is really dependent on how confident you feel stitching the ditch. (I'll be honest: I actually really would hand-stitch this. It might take me three months of wishing I'd finished it to finally get around to it, but I know every time I put the dress on I'd be glad I did. Any of the three handstitches described on page 122 will work; slipstitch is the standard, but whipstitch is my favorite.)

8. TOPSTITCH STRAPS

To secure the straps, you can either topstitch across the upper edge of the bodice, or you can hand-stitch each strap in place at the upper edge. If you choose to do an invisible hem, as shown below, I'd opt for the hand-stitching, just to keep everything on the same playing field.

Hem the Skirt

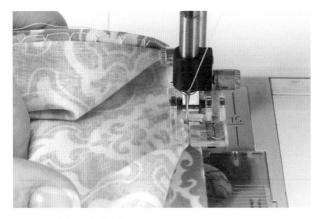

STITCH INVISIBLE HEM

To create an invisible hem, begin by pressing up ¼" (6.4mm) all along the lower edge of the skirt. Then, press another ½" (1.3cm) all the way around, steaming to ease out any fullness as you do. Look at the skirt with the hem turned to the inside. Now, gripping both pressed edges, flip the whole hem to the outside, so the pressed sections are right sides together with the outside of the skirt. Pinch the hem so that a teeny bit of the inner fold—the ¼" (6.4mm) one—is peeking out beyond the fold of the skirt (you'll see the wrong side of the skirt interior here). Using an invisible hem foot, set your machine to an invisible hem stitch—it looks a lot like a heart rate monitor. When you sew, the straight stitches should fall on the pressed portion—the hem allowance—and the "hiccup" stitches should catch just a thread or two of the skirt interior. Continue around the entire hem until it's all in place, then steam and press from the right side to set the stitches and make them really invisible!

The pockets here are on-seam, and a slight variation can produce the delightful peekaboo pockets of the **Sassy Pants** (see page 196).

Nothing says sundress like a nice picnic. Move to the **Fabric Picnic Basket** (see page 106) as your next step, and be ready for any spring afternoon in the grass!

Vintage charm oozes from this dress. I love the idea of using a vintage photo for the **Photo-Transfer Wall Art** (see page 36)—move on to that as your next step and get a theme going!

NEXT STEPS

TRY THIS, TOO: GO STRAPLESS

For an evening version of this dress, think about going strapless. Follow the same steps we outlined here, but skip the stuff about the straps. Also, fold the upper edge down to make a "cuff" at the neckline, kinda like Marty's mom's dress at the Under the Sea Dance in *Back to the Future*.

LEVEL 4 | SASSY PANTS

I feel like I spend half my life looking for just the right pants: not too high in the rise (but not too low), not too skinny in the leg (but not too wide), not too bulky at the waist (but with some support) and suitable for pairing with tees when it's casual and snazzy jackets when it's not. I think I may have hit the mother lode with this pattern, and am pretty sure I won't be making another style of pant anytime soon. With a faced waistline, instead of a waistband, these lie flat below your navel for a streamlined look. Semi-fitted through the hip and thigh, they make you look narrower and accent only the best parts of your curve, but the full zip fly is as perfectly useful as it is easy to install. Finally: Sew some REAL pants, and then actually wear them out of the house. With everything. (Ahem. Might I suggest pairing them with the knit top and sassy jacket in this very tome?)

SUPPLIES

2–2½ yds (1.8 m–2.3 m) of bottom weight fabric like denim, twill or wool

½ yd (1.46 m) of fusible interfacing

5"–7" (12.7 cm-17.8 cm) metal pants zipper

Hook-and-eye closure

Matching thread

Cut Fabric

SELVAGE

FRONT · POCKET · POCKET FACING · FRONT WAISTBAND

FLY · BACK · BACK WAISTBAND · FLY FACING

FOLD

CUT PIECES

Cut all the pants pattern pieces from your fabric, taking care to pay attention to notches: pants front (2), pants back (2), pocket lining (2), pocket (2), waistband back (1 on fold), waistband front (2). Transfer all markings for darts to the wrong side of your fabric.

INTERFACE

Interface the front and back facings before you begin.

THE IMPORTANCE OF MAKING A MUSLIN

There has been a ton of talk in the crafting community about "making a muslin," and not everyone really even knows what that means. Basically, before you go sewing with your $190/yard lace, you want to do a trial run and make sure your design will work. Enter the muslin: Made with inexpensive fabric that mimics the drape and weight of your fancy fabric, you can practice your design and modifications before you cut into the Good Stuff. For pants, especially, the value of making a muslin can't be overstated. It really gives you an opportunity to test the fit and your technique without using up your very most favorite hoarded fabric. Because everyone's body is different, and everyone likes to wear their pants at different places on their hip, no pants pattern will be perfectly perfect for you unless you try it out and see what you love and don't love. Consider making a "wearable muslin," meaning make a test run out of inexpensive fabric (or stash fabric) you would be willing to wear if all goes well. That way: You get to practice, but you don't get nagged by guilt at the idea of wasting all that time and effort!

Facings and Darts

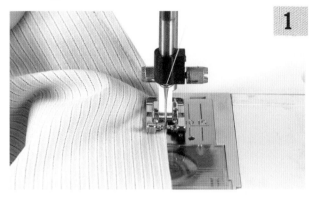

1. STITCH BACK DARTS

Stitch the back darts. Remember, always begin sewing a dart at the larger end, heading toward the point, and don't backtack. (See page 182 for the Crash Course on darts.) Press toward the center back.

2. STITCH UNDERLAP TOGETHER; FINISH STRAIGHT EDGE

Place two underlap pieces right sides together. Sew a ⅝" (1.6cm) seam allowance along the curved edge. Grade the seam allowance (see below). Clip curves, turn right-side out and press savagely.

With the underlap curving to the left, finish the raw straight edge by trimming the top layer ¼" (6.4mm), then folding the upper layer back over the trimmed edge and stitching in place.

GRADING A SEAM ALLOWANCE

Grading simply means to take the seam allowance to levels that will taper off slowly rather than jump off like a cliff. When all your seam allowances are the same width, and you have a bulkier fabric or seam, they can make a ridge that is visible through the garment—and it doesn't look very nice or very professional. By grading the seam allowance, you basically terrace the edges of the fabric in order to gradually decrease the thickness to avoid that big lump at your seamline. Do this by trimming away a bit of the seam allowance on one thickness of fabric, then a bit more on the next, and on until all the layers of seam allowance at a particular seam are trimmed to descending widths. Take care that the narrowest seam allowance is at least ¼" (6.4mm) and you're golden!

Zip Fly

Switch to your zipper foot before starting the zip fly.

1. STITCH FLY TO PANTS FRONT

Working with the left pants front, place the fly and pants front right sides together. Stitch a ⅝" (1.6cm) seam allowance from the upper edge to the dot. Grade the seam allowances. Press the fly away from the pants front, and the seam allowances toward the fly.

2. PIN ZIPPER TO PANTS

Place the zipper facedown on the left side of the fly and line up the lower edge of the zipper tape with the circle. If the upper end of the zipper hangs off the fabric, no worries, but the lower edge of zip tape must be at the circle to correctly place the zip stop. Place the edge of the zipper with right zipper tape even with the seamline. Pin in place.

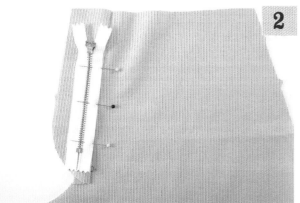

3. BASTE ZIPPER IN PLACE

To stabilize the zipper and center it on the seam, baste it in place using your zipper foot, along the left zipper tape.

4. STITCH

Move the needle to the right of the zipper foot OR switch zipper foot to opposite side, if your zipper foot has two bars to attach it to the ankle, and stitch the left zipper tape in place close to the teeth. Stitch again, about ¼" (6.4mm) away from the first line of stitching. Sew the seams until you run out of fly fabric to stitch or get to the end of the tape.

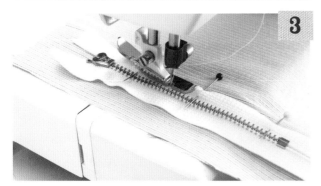

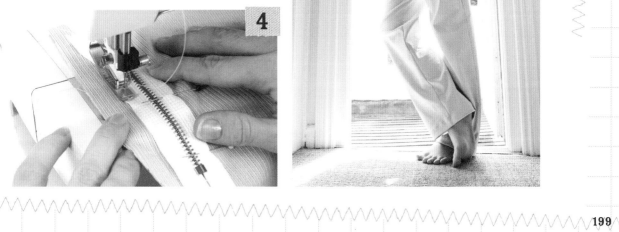

5. PULL ASIDE RIGHT ZIPPER TAPE

Fold the fly back to the wrong side along the original seamline. Press. Pull the right zipper tape aside and pin it up and out of the way; you'll need it to be free for the next few steps.

6. BASTE FLY

From the wrong side, baste the fly in place using the edge of the curved piece as a guide.

7. TOPSTITCH FLY

From the right side, topstitch the fly in place along the dotted line, stopping and backtacking at the center front, still keeping the right zipper tape free.

8. REMOVE ZIPPER BASTING

Remove the basting at the right zipper tape. Set the left pants front aside.

9. CLIP AND FOLD SEAM ALLOWANCE

On the right pants front, clip into the seam allowance at the circle on the center front edge ⅜" (9.5cm). Fold back to the wrong side from circle to the waistline along the center front ⅜" (9.5cm) and press in place.

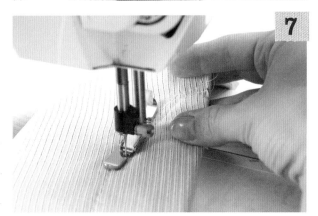

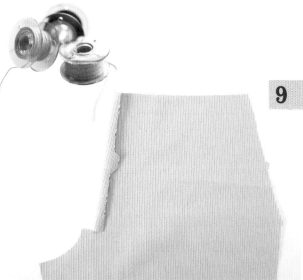

10. STITCH RIGHT ZIPPER TAPE

Line the folded left front pants edge up with the zipper teeth on the right zipper tape. Open the right zipper tape to stitch. Baste from the bottom to the top, then zip closed to check its function.

11. PLACE UNDERLAP

Place the right zipper under the notched edge of the underlap. On the wrong side, place the curve of the underlap to mirror the curve of the topstitching.

12. BASTE

Baste in place.

13. STITCH CROTCH SEAM

Place the left pants front and right pants front right sides together. Stitch the crotch seam from dot to inseam.

14. PINCH ZIPPER TAPE; STITCH

Pinch the zipper tapes together to allow access to the dot (shown here); leaving an opening here can create a draft! From the right side, use the zipper foot to stitch through all the layers from top to bottom with the zipper open and the fly front free. Pull threads to the back and tie a knot to secure.

15. STITCH A BAR TACK

Set your machine to a zigzag with a stitch length of zero. At the base of the zipper stop, stitch a bar tack by sewing back and forth three or four times. This will reinforce the seam close to the bottom of the zipper.

16. FINISH ZIPPER

Open the zipper. At the upper edge of the zipper, remove any extra teeth. Baste across the upper edge of the pants to secure the zipper tapes in place.

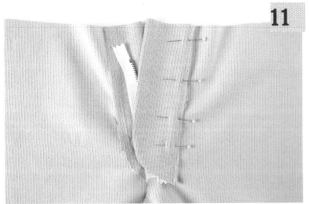

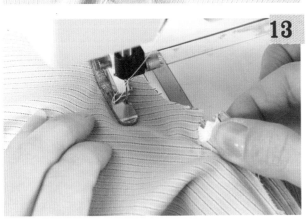

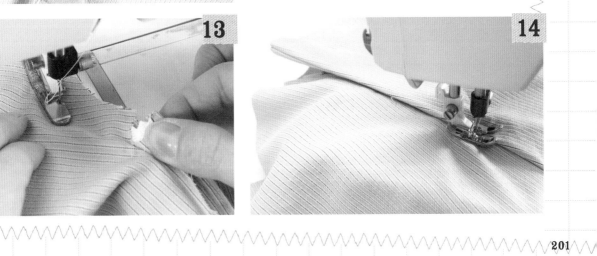

Crotch and Inseam

1. STITCH CENTER BACK SEAM

Place the pants backs right sides together. Stitch the center back seam. If you're finishing your seams with pinking shears or with a serger, do that after each seam is stitched.

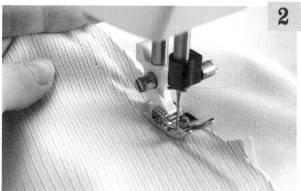

2. SEW INSEAM

Place the pants front and pants back together, matching the crotch seam. Sew the inseam from hem to hem. Press open.

Pockets and Side Seam

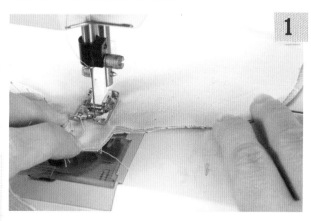

1. ATTACH POCKET

Attach the pocket right sides together to the pants front, matching the notches. Sew a ⅝" (1.6cm) seam allowance.

Press the pocket to the outside, then understitch the seam. Understitching works to attach the lining or facing to the seam allowances so that it is less likely to roll outward. Do this by opening out the seam, folding the seam allowances toward the facings, and stitching through all three thicknesses.

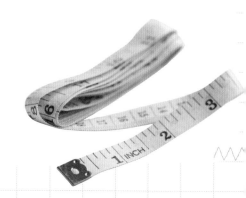

2. STITCH POCKET CURVE

Place the pants front right sides together with the pocket, matching the notches and raw edges. Stitch around the pocket curve, ending at the seamline.

3. SEW SIDE SEAMS

Fold the pocket back to the wrong side, lining up the raw edge of the pants side front and pants front to create a new edge for the side seam. Sew the side seam from waist to hem

    Repeat steps 2-3 on the opposite side.

4. STITCH WAISTBAND FACING PIECES TOGETHER

Sew each interfaced waistband facing piece at the side seams to create a single waistline facing. Use an overcast stitch on the lower edge of facings.

5. PRESS FACING EDGES; STITCH SEAM

Press under the front edges of the facing by ¾" (1.9cm). Place it right sides together with the pants, matching the side seams. The folded ends of the facing should come on one side to stop at the zipper teeth, and at the other all the way to overlap the fly opening. Stitch using a ⅝" (1.6cm) seam allowance, leaving the upper edges of the fly shield free.

6. CONCEAL FLY FACING

With the facing stitched in place, tuck in the upper raw edges of the fly facing so that they're concealed inside the facing itself. You'll need to tuck away about ¼" (6.4mm) on each side. Stitch across this fold.

7. TURN FACING; STITCH WAISTLINE EDGE

Turn the facing to the inside and press it in place. Stitch around the waistline edge approximately 1" (2.5cm) from the upper seam. Stitch through all the layers, all the way to the front of the pants.

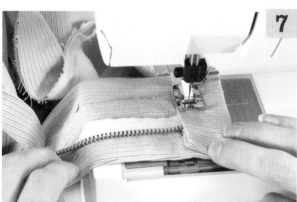

8. HEM LEGS

At the lower edge of each pants leg, turn under ¼" (6.4mm) and press. Turn under another ½" (1.3cm) and press again. Take it to the machine and stitch through all layers, close to the inner fold to hem.

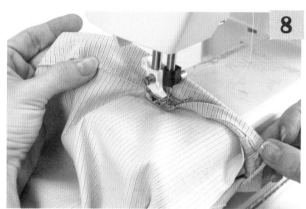

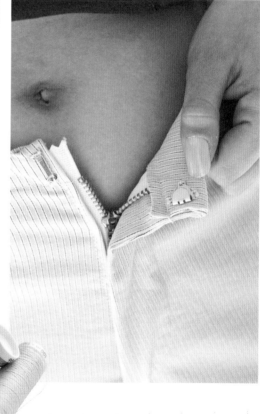

TRY THIS, TOO!

Experiment with different types of fabric. Suiting fabrics work great, and can really dress these pants up!

Putting in hems is a skill that develops over the course of making many garments. After working on the hems here, try the **Knit Top** (see page 172) and see the variation when hemming another type of fabric.

Kick it up a notch in these pants when you make them in an unexpected fabric and combine them with the **Beaded Evening Clutch** (see page 124). Plus, you'll find that the skills you used to create the fly here translate themselves very well to manipulating the fabric of the clutch into the frame!

NEXT
STEPS

LEVEL 5 | WHEREVER JACKET

Very few garments can be as universally useful as a good, fitted jacket. It dresses up the most casual of outfits and instantly takes you from soccer-mom-in-the-carpool-line to chic-and-classy-mom-who-always-looks-great-no-matter-what. Make it in simple fabrics to wear all the time, or in truly special fabrics to take every outfit up a notch. Put it over dresses, skirts, pants, leggings, you name it. Give it piping, as in the variation, or leave it off—you're the lady who's about to have a whole closetful of these bad boys, so get ready to mix it up.

SUPPLIES

2½ yds (2.3 m) of heavy fabric, like corduroy, wool or twill

1 yd (0.91 m) of coordinating lighter weight cotton made into 2" (5 cm) single fold bias tape

Three 1" (2.5 cm) buttons

Matching thread

½ yd (0.46 m) of midweight fusible interfacing

Cut and Interface

1. CUTTING

Cut all pattern pieces: jacket front (2), jacket back (2), sleeve (2, one right and one left), upper collar (1), lower collar (1), collar stand (2), front facings (2, one right and one left).

All are cut from the same fabric. When cutting the front facings, you can either print the pattern piece for the jacket front twice, and in one of them trim with your paper scissors along the line that says "cut here for front facing," or you can lay out the jacket front pattern piece when you're ready to cut your facing and lift the edge slightly to allow you to trim just under that line on the paper, as shown in the photo.

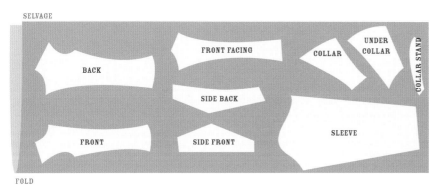

2. INTERFACING

Apply the fusible interfacing to the jacket right and left front facings. Repeat with the under collar.

Jacket Front and Back

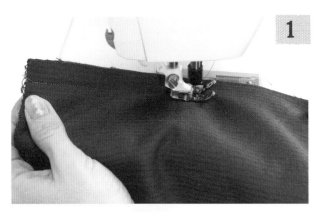

1. STAYSTITCH NECKLINE; STITCH CENTER BACK

Staystitch the neckline edge between notches. Then stitch the center back seam. Don't bother pressing open—you're gonna finish this off with bias tape, so you don't need to! Huzzah!

2. TRIM SEAM AND PREPARE BIAS TAPE

Trim the center back seam down to ¼" (6.4mm). Then prepare your ⅜" (9.5mm) double-fold bias tape; either purchase some store-bought or make your own continuous bias tape. If you make your own, press in each edge using a bias tape maker, and then press again in half.

3. BIND SEAM

To bind each seam as you work through this jacket, you'll wrap the seam allowance with the bias tape, setting the edge of the seam allowance right in the fold of the bias tape. You can pin in place, but I generally pinch it firmly in my fingers and then take it to the machine to stitch. Stitch through all three layers, close to the original seam line, taking care to catch the fold of the bias tape on the back. When you're finished, you have a clean seam that's completely covered in bias tape, looks great even on the inside of the garment and will never unravel.

4. STITCH SIDE BACK/FRONT AND JACKET BACK/FRONT

Stitch the side back to the jacket back using a ⅝" (1.6cm) seam allowance. Repeat with the jacket fronts and jacket side fronts, taking care with each of these seams to finish the seam allowance with bias tape, as you did on the jacket center back.

5. PRESS SEAM FLAT

When the seams are all bound in bias tape, press each one nice and flat. The side back and side front seams should all be pressed flat and toward the center of the jacket.

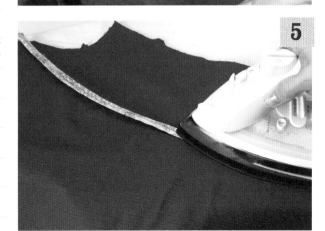

6. STITCH FRONT TO BACK

Stitch the jacket fronts to the jacket back at the shoulder seams and side seams, with right sides together and a ⅝" (1.6cm) seam allowance.

FRENCH SEAMS VS. BIAS-BOUND SEAMS

As you make this jacket, you're binding each seam in bias tape to create an unlined jacket that is clean and finished on the inside, with no visible seam allowances. An alternate technique for achieving the same result is the French seam. French seams encase the seam allowance within them, so rather than adding another fabric to encase the seam, you're doing it with the fabric itself. It can be lovely, but takes pre-planning and careful pressing to make it successful. Begin by sewing each seam at ¼" (6.4mm) with the fabrics WRONG sides together. Then, when the seam is done, trim the seam allowances down to a scant ¼" (6.4mm). Press the seam with the fabrics RIGHT sides together, very crisp. Then stitch another seam on the desired finished seamline—that is, at ⅜" (9.5mm), catching the seam allowances inside the second seam. You'll have a very clean finish! This technique works best with lighter-weight fabrics, like linens and silks, and doesn't do as well with bulkier wools and blends.

Under Collar

1. REINFORCE COLLAR NOTCH

Reinforce the notch on the collar edge by sewing to the large dot, pivoting and sewing past the dot on the other side. Clip to the circle, up to but not through the stitching.

2. STITCH UNDER COLLAR TO NECKLINE

Stitch the under collar sections at the center back. Press the seam allowances open. Place the under collar at the neckline edge, matching the notches and center seams. Clip the edge of the neckline if necessary to ease in the fullness.

3. STITCH AND TRIM

Stitch between the large circles and pivot at the small circles. Trim the seam allowances.

Sleeves

Unlike the two-part sleeve on the boy's jacket in the previous chapter, we'll be making this sleeve an inset sleeve, which means we want to make the sleeve itself into a tube before we insert it into the armhole opening.

1. ADD EASE STITCHES; STITCH UNDERARM SEAM

Sew ease stitches at the upper curve of the shoulder, using your longest straight stitch. Sew another row ¼" (6.4mm) to the inside of that.

Stitch the underarm seam right sides together. Press the seam allowances open.

2. PLACE SLEEVE IN ARMHOLE

Place the sleeve in the armhole with the sleeve right-side out and the jacket wrong-side out. Pin in place. Adjust the ease by manipulating the ease stitches, drawing up excess volume until the two lie right inside one another. Match notches to make sure you've got the correct sleeve on

the correct side! Single notch means front, double notch means back.

3. STITCH

Stitch a ⅝" (1.6cm) seam allowance, and another at ⅜" (9.5mm). Trim the seam allowance. Press the seam toward sleeve.

Repeat this process for the other sleeve.

4. BIND SEAM ALLOWANCES

Trim the seam allowances on each sleeve hole, and then bind with bias tape as you did the other seams. While those seams can remain open at each end, since we'll catch them later, here you'll want to fold in one end of the bias tape and use it to finish off the binding when your stitches return to where they began.

Collar and Front Facings

1. MAKE UPPER COLLAR

Create the upper collar as you did the under collar (see page 209, step 3), stitching the collar band along the edge of the collar piece.

2. FINISH

On the front facing, use bias tape to finish off the interior curved edge from across the upper short section then down the curve to the hemline. Then place the facing right sides together with the upper collar and collar band, using the upper curve to the point on the facing. Pin along the raw edge, keeping the two shapes aligned. Repeat on the opposite facing.

3. FINISH OFF FACING UPPER EDGE

Take a small piece of bias tape and place it across the neckline edge where the facings do not cover the raw edge of the jacket back. Open out the folds and place raw edge to raw edge, sandwiching the upper edge of the facings between the bias tape and the jacket body.

Stitch across both facings and the edge of the bias tape at the collar band neckline using a ⅝" (1.6cm) seam allowance. Press the seam allowances toward the collar band.

4. STITCH FACING AND UPPER COLLAR

Place the facing and upper collar together with the outer jacket, right sides touching. Match all the notches and circles. Stitch from the lower front edge to the lower front edge, across the collar. Stitches should extend to the curve at the base of the facing. Be sure to backtack when you get there! Trim the seam allowances. When you come to the notch where you reinforced the collar sections, stop and backstitch. Then, moving the seam allowances out of the way to the other side, begin a new seam, backstitch and complete sewing. This will free those seam allowances so they'll lie flat for you later.

5. CLIP CURVES, TRIM SEAMS; TURN AND TOPSTITCH

Clip the curve at the base of the jacket to allow you to get a smooth finish when you turn it right-side out. Trim the seam allowances just on this curved portion to ¼" (6.4mm).

Turn right-side out. Press all seams smooth. Topstitch from the lower edge to the lower edge, across the collar.

6. CLIP POINTS

At the collar points, clip the point, then trim the seam allowances at an angle to reduce the bulk.

Hem the Jacket

ADD BIAS TAPE TO HEM; TOPSTITCH

To hem the jacket, turn the facings back to the wrong side. Apply a piece of bias tape to the hemline edge, just as you've done previously. The raw ends of the bias tape should overlap the facing edges. Stitch using a ½" (1.3cm) seam allowance. Turn the facings to the right side again, and see how the bias tape gets flipped up into place to serve as a hem tape. Pin this in place, with the folded edge tucked under. Topstitch the entire edge of the jacket, from the bias tape hem, across the facings, over the collar—taking care to pivot at the points—then down the other side and back to the hem, overlapping your stitches with where you began just slightly.

Buttons and Buttonholes

Add three buttons on the front of this jacket to get that classic tailored look. Use 1" (2.5cm) or 1¼" (3.2cm) buttons, and try on the jacket to check the placement—the markings on the pattern piece will guide you, but you'll want to be sure that the top-most button holds the jacket along your bustline to get the fabric to hang just right.

1. STITCH BUTTONHOLES

Using the markings on the pattern pieces, set the buttonholes and stitch them in place. Clip open the holes. (See the Crash Course on buttonholes on page 169 as needed.)

2. ADD BUTTONS

Add buttons with a shank, using the marks on the pattern as a guide.

TRY THIS, TOO!

This jacket works so well in any fabric, but I highly recommend the experience of sewing with the best fabrics you can—you'll love both the process and the product so much more. See if you can't score a really great wool tweed (check the resources section in the back for ideas of where to begin), and fall in love with this classic fabric that sews up so beautifully.

The binding you use on the interior seams of this jacket is bias tape—which I recommend for the binding of your **Sewing Machine Cover** (see page 64). Such different applications, but the same skill for each!

Working on this jacket is a reminder of how a shaped or curved seam can really affect the overall performance of a garment—or any sewn object. Try the same approach by making the **Tea Cozy** next (see page 76), where curved seams create an entirely unexpected shape for the project.

When you complete a challenging project, sometimes the best next step is to go back to the basics and take a rest. Move to the **Ribboned Envelope Pillow** next (see page 16) and remind yourself how soothing straight seams can be.

NEXT STEPS

CONCLUSION

Learning to sew isn't something you do once and never do again. It's a skill, yes, but it's also an art and more. When you first touch a sewing machine, it seems like a completely foreign world, but I think most of us quickly learn that it's way more than that.

There is something transformative about sewing, something that allows us to take ourselves out of our daily lives, forget our worries and escape to something bigger. While the project you're working on might seem small, when you put needle to fabric, you are part of something that began long before you learned to sew, and will continue long after, a trajectory of imagination and creation that ties you to women you have never met but who share something with you. Sewing can allow you to both dream and realize, to imagine and create, to leap and to land. It is truly something unique and special, and like opera, can ignite a fire in your soul that you didn't know you lacked, but that burns bright and illuminates you and everything in your path.

I realize I'm going all hyperbole here, but the excitement and fulfillment I feel when I sew is unparalleled, and something I treasure and hold dear. Once you learn to use your machine and work with various fabrics, there is nothing you can't learn and make! You have the power!!

Rock on, Little Stitcher, and set forth in this brave new world to make and become.

HOW TO USE THE CD AND PATTERNS

You'll find the following pattern files on the CD:

Tea Cozy
Everyday Shoulder Bag
Beaded Evening Clutch
Lovie Blanket
Knit Top
Enchantment Under the Sea Dress
Wherever Jacket

Whole Cloth Quilt Designs
Classy Lady Elbow Bag
Reversible Girl's Dress
Boy's Lined Pea Coat
A-Line Skirt with Peekaboo Pleat
Sassy Pants

The format of the patterns included on the CD is slightly different than what you might be expecting, and there are some reasons for that.

First, I've met so many new stitchers who feel intimidated by a tissue paper pattern, the kind that comes in the envelope from the fabric shop. Their fear is that they'll cut it out wrong and ruin the pattern forever, and it gives them a kind of deer-in-headlights feeling as they approach a project. Since I would vastly prefer that you jump in and discover you can do a lot more than you think you can, I really wanted these patterns to have a different format, one that would eliminate that concern by allowing you to print them over and over, and make mistakes without worry.

Second, there are so many new pattern resources out there (and a bunch of them are listed in the Resources section of the book) that use downloadable patterns, most of them free of charge. Yippee! But what if you've only ever used tissue patterns and the free ones look so strange to you that you're prevented from really taking advantage of all the great stuff that's out there, the really modern, edgy stuff that appeals to you most?

So the patterns are all presented in a PDF format and tiled. What that means is that each pattern piece is larger than a single sheet of 8½" × 11" (22cm × 28cm) printer paper, but to help you print them on a regular printer, they are split on multiple sheets. Your job is to print them out and then put them together. The benefit is that you can repeat this procedure over and over, and avoid needing to store a pattern (unless you choose) while also knowing that if you do make a mistake, it's a snap to fix!

Insert the CD into your computer, and open the PDF patterns using Adobe Acrobat Reader (this software can be downloaded free of charge on the internet). Note that if you want, you can send these files electronically to a print shop and have them printed on a single, large-format page.

When assembling the patterns, match the letters along the edge of each page with the same letter on the adjoining page. Once you have the pages matched with their neighbors, overlap each page slightly until the star along the page edge is re-assembled—you'll notice that the star or triangle is printed on the edge of both pages, and by overlapping the edges and lining up the edges of the star or triangle you'll reassemble the pattern with no gaps or skips in the design lines. Tape along the edges to secure using clear tape or painter's tape (you might want to focus your tape within the lines of each pattern piece, so that when you cut the pattern pieces from the paper they will remain intact). Once you have all the pattern pieces cut out, pin or weight on your fabric and cut!

RESOURCES AND INSPIRATION

Here are some of my favorite reference and inspiration books:

The Sewing Bible by Ruth Singer: Gorgeously photographed and with clear instructions. Covers a huge range of techniques, with some small projects at the back that, while they seem like a bit of an afterthought, are very pretty and inspiring.

The Sewing Book by Alison Smith: A Dorling-Kindersley book, so it's stunningly photographed. Another wide-ranging reference. Gives you plenty of techniques to learn or apply, but no instruction as to where to use them. I like that it inspires me to find projects on which to try new skills!

Vogue/Butterick Step-by-Step Guide to Sewing Techniques: Illustrated in a manner very similar to their sewing pattern instructions, this is a handy reference to have on the shelf for any time you get stuck in constructing a project from a store-bought pattern, as it allows you to decipher some of the less-than-well-written instructions.

Vogue Sewing: Very similar to the title above, but this one has a fabulous introductory section that covers body style, flattering design, how to measure, pattern alterations, and then launches into the skills in clear sections with ideas for application.

Reader's Guide Complete Guide to Sewing: My could-not-live-without reference, for reals. Every technique under the sun, fantastic instruction and illustration. Makes no effort to teach you when and where to use the techniques, so this one is strictly a reference, but it's endlessly useful. It is essential that you get a copy published prior to 1974—all the later editions cut out up to 100+ pages of the text and add little of value.

Modern Quilts, Traditional Inspiration by Denyse Schmidt: From the widely-recognized mother of the "new quilting," a beautiful book that covers quilting basics (and beyond) in modern style.

The Art of Manipulating Fabric by Colette Wolff: This one could probably go under encyclopedic references, but since it deals strictly with how to fold, gather, roll, or otherwise alter the fabric itself, it's really a specialized book. I love flipping through and seeing the hundreds of techniques all modeled in simple muslin, so you really get an idea of how the fabric of your project itself can be changed.

Stitch by Stitch by Deborah Moebes: Shameless self-serving promotion? Probably. But I do honestly and sincerely believe that it's the best way to learn to sew: with projects that will give you enough instant gratification to stay motivated, and that teach skills that build upon one another.

The Gentle Art of Domesticity by Jane Brocket: Beautiful photos and lovely philosophy on the art of sewing and creating for yourself, those you love, and the home you share.

Sewing A to Z by Nancy Zieman: One of the foremost experts on sewing currently working today, Nancy Zieman presents a wide-ranging reference with answers to nearly any sewing question you can think to ask. With pictures!

BLOGS I LOVE

Made By Rae www.made-by-rae.com
MADE www.danamadeit.com
Gertie's New Blog for Better Sewing www.blogforbettersewing.com
Sew, Mama, Sew www.sewmamasew.com
Whipstitch www.whip-stitch.com
Burda Style www.burdastyle.com/patterns
Fehr Trade www.fehrtrade.com
The Selfish Seamstress www.selfishseamstress.wordpress.com
Lizzy House www.lizzyhouse.typepad.com
Anna Maria Horner www.annamariahorner.blogspot.com
Colette Patterns www.coletterie.com
True Up (all fabric, all the time) www.trueup.com

FABRIC SOURCES

Fabric Mart Fabrics www.fabricmartfabrics.com
Pink Chalk Fabrics www.pinkchalkfabrics.com
Hawthorne Threads www.hawthornethreads.com
Fabric Depot www.fabricdepot.com
FaFabricsStore.com (great source for affordable, good-quality linen)
www.fabrics-store.com
Martha Pullen www.marthapullen.com

NOTIONS & SUPPLIES FOR THE PROJECTS

Fabric.com: Some home dec notions, small selection of hardware
www.fabric.com
Atlanta Thread Supply: Huge selection of even the most obscure
notions and tools store.
Major chain stores, including Jo-Ann and Hancock: Probably less fun to
shop than the smaller stores and independent shops, but easily accessible.
You've almost certainly got one within 100 miles of you, and they're also online.

INDEX

ABOUT THE AUTHOR

Deborah Moebes writes Whipstitch, a blog about modern sewing. After a decade as a schoolteacher and a short career as an archaeologist, Deborah stumbled (kinda backward) into sewing and has never looked back. She's the owner of a popular sewing lounge in Atlanta, designs sewing patterns, teaches sewing classes in person and online and is a regular speaker at sewing events and conferences.

She also has four kids, a husband, a (lovely but largely imagined) garden, a fantastic mid-century modern ranch (which is the subject of many a Pinterest post and on-going DIY renovation), a dog and (soon to be, if the children get their way) two fish. She firmly believes that sewing is for everyone, and that you'll learn the most if you jump in with both feet and give it a shot–even if you're not quite sure what you're doing. She is also quite adamant that everything ought to have pockets. Currently, Deborah is polishing up a new crop of garment patterns, sewing almost constantly for her new house and working her way through a wall quilt featuring Tony Danza.

Visit Deborah at **www.whip-stitch.com.**

Dedication:

This book is for Emma, whose sewing lessons always got delayed. In one way or another, you are in every one of these projects.

Acknowledgements: This book was a tremendous labor of love, and there are a lot of hands on it who should be thanked profusely. Giant shout-out to Vanessa Lyman, editor extraordinaire, who brought this ship into port—couldn't have done it without you, and wouldn't have been here without you, anyway. To my other editors along the way: Bethany, Kristin (back for Round 2!), Rachel and Julie, you've each shaped this book as it developed, and I'm so grateful that you were there to give me guidance. And tissues. Mega-massive thanks to Christine Polomsky, greatest step-by-step photographer on the planet—it was an honor to work with you again. Thanks to Sarah Underhill for all her gorgeous design work—I love the look of this book, and love that you were so willing to work with me to get it right. To my mom, who always had an ear and loving words when the work got tough. To my children, who put up with a loooot of late nights. And most of all, to my husband, who never for an instant doubted that I could do it, and it would be amazing—you're the best man in the world, and I am so proud to be your wife.

METRIC CONVERSION CHART

TO CONVERT		TO		MULTIPLY BY
Inches	>	Centimeters	>	2.54
Centimeters	>	Inches	>	0.4
Feet	>	Centimeters	>	30.5
Centimeters	>	Feet	>	0.03
Yards	>	Meters	>	0.9
Meters	>	Yards	>	1.1

The technique and base design for "Improvisational Landscape Wall Quilt" on page 90 are used by permission from Sherri Lynn Wood from her "Mod Mood Quilt" tutorial (http://daintytime.net/2010/06/05/modern-mood-quilt-craft-along/). All rights reserved.

www.fwmedia.com

16 15 14 13 12   5 4 3 2 1

Distributed in Canada by Fraser Direct
100 Armstrong Avenue
Georgetown, ON, Canada L7G 5S4
Tel: (905) 877-4411

Distributed in the U.K. and Europe by F&W MEDIA INTERNATIONAL
Brunel House, Newton Abbot, Devon, TQ12 4PU, England
Tel: (+44) 1626 323200, Fax: (+44) 1626 323319
Email: enquiries@fwmedia.com

Distributed in Australia by Capricorn Link
P.O. Box 704, S. Windsor NSW, 2756 Australia
Tel: (02) 4577-3555

SRN: W7260
ISBN-13: 978-1-4402-2947-3

Editor: Rachel Scheller, Bethany Anderson, Kristin Boys
Designer: Sarah Underhill
Production Coordinator: Greg Nock
Photographers: Bangwallop Photography

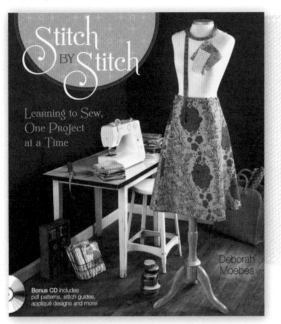

Even more projects and inspiration! Huzzah!

If you've taken a notion to sew, come find more inspiring books, fabrics, tools and so much more at **Store.MarthaPullen.com!**

Stitch by Stitch: Learning to Sew, One Project at a Time
Check out Deborah's first book, the best-est introduction to sewing ever. In *Stitch by Stitch*, she gives you all the instructions you need to sew your way through 11 stylish projects. Includes PDF patterns on CD-rom.

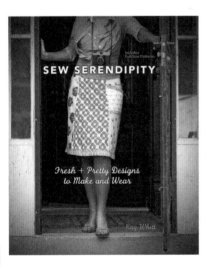

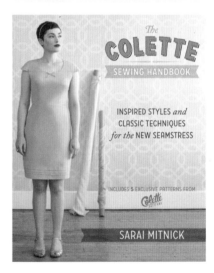

Sew Serendipity: Fresh + Pretty Designs to Make and Wear
Check out Kay Whitt's first book for easy-to-make skirts, tunic dresses and jackets. A customized wardrobe is just a needle-and-thread away! Includes full-size pattern sheets.

Sew Serendipity Bags: Fresh + Pretty Projects to Sew and Love
With full instructions for twelve bags—and with a few clever variations thrown in—there are plenty of designs to choose from! Includes full-size pattern sheets.

The Colette Sewing Handbook: Inspired Styles and Classic Techniques for the New Seamstress
Five simple fundamentals can help you perfect any sewing project: a thoughtful plan, a precise pattern, a fantastic fit, a beautiful fabric, and a fine finish. With these five core ideas, *The Colette Sewing Handbook* shows you how to start sewing the wardrobe of your dreams.